D0554528

RENEWALS 691-4574
DATE DUE

DEC 11			
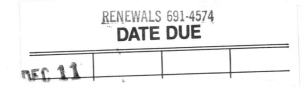

WITHDRAWN
UTSA Libraries

HISTORY OF
THE BYZANTINE
EMPIRE

HISTORY OF THE
Byzantine Empire

BY CHARLES DIEHL

TRANSLATED FROM THE FRENCH
BY GEORGE B. IVES

AMS PRESS
NEW YORK

LIBRARY
University of Texas
At San Antonio

Reprinted from the edition of 1925, Princeton
First AMS EDITION published 1969
Manufactured in the United States of America

Library of Congress Catalogue Card Number: 76-91295

AMS PRESS, INC.
NEW YORK, N.Y. 10003

LIBRARY
University of Texas
At San Antonio

PREFACE

THE *history of the Byzantine Empire, notwith-standing the numerous works which have almost re-created it in the last fifty years, is still the object of un-yielding prejudices, especially in the West. To many of our contemporaries it still appears, as it appeared to Montesquieu and Gibbon, as the continuation and de-generation of the Roman Empire. Through an uncon-scious effect of immemorial jealousies, through a dim recollection of vanished religious passions, we still judge the Greeks of the Middle Ages as did the Crusaders, who did not understand them, and the Popes, who excom-municated them.*

In like manner, Byzantine art is still too often re-garded as a stationary art,— we like to call it "hieratic," — powerless to renew itself, and, under the close surveil-lance of the Church, limiting its thousand-year activity to copying over and over again the creations of a few artists of genius.

As a matter of fact, Byzantium was something quite different. Although she freely proclaimed herself to be the inheritor and continuator of Rome; although her emper-ors, to the very last, assumed the title of "Basileus of the Romans"; although they never abandoned the claims that they asserted to the ancient and glorious capital of the Empire, yet in reality Byzantium very quickly be-came, and was essentially, an Oriental monarchy.

v

PREFACE

It must not be judged by comparison with the over-whelming memories of Rome: in the words of one of the men who has best understood its character and seen it in its true aspect, it was "a mediæval state, situated on the extreme frontier of Europe, on the confines of Asiatic barbarism."[1] *This state had its defects and its vices, which it would be puerile to attempt to conceal. It too often experienced palace revolutions and military seditions; it was tremendously fond of the games of the circus, and still fonder of theological disputes; despite the refinement of its civilization, its customs were often cruel and barbarous; and, lastly, it produced in too great abundance mediocre characters and base souls. But, such as it was, this state was great.*

Nor should we imagine, as we are only too prone to do, that Byzantium declined uninterruptedly toward destruction during the thousand years that she survived the fall of the Roman Empire. The critical periods in which she was near collapse were followed again and again by periods of incomparable splendor, by unexpected regenerations, when, in the words of a chronicler, "the empire, old woman that she is, appears like a young girl, adorned with gold and precious stones."

In the sixth century, under Justinian, for the last time the Empire was reconstructed as in the glorious days of Rome, and the Mediterranean again became a Roman lake. In the eighth century, the Isaurian emperors checked the onrush of Islam, at about the same time that Charles Martel saved Christendom at Poitiers. In the tenth century, the rulers of the Macedonian dynasty made Byzantium the great power of the Orient, carrying

[1] A. Rambaud, *L'Empire Grec, au Xme siècle*, p. vii.

their victorious arms even into Syria, crushing the Russians on the Danube, drowning in blood the kingdom created by the Bulgarian tsars. In the twelfth century, under the Comneni, the Greek Empire still made a respectable figure in the world, and Constantinople was one of the principal centers of European polity.

Thus, for a thousand years, Byzantium lived; and not merely as the result of a fortunate hazard; she lived gloriously; and that it should be so, she must have had within her something besides vices. To direct her affairs she had great emperors, illustrious statesmen, skilful diplomats, and victorious generals; and through them she accomplished a great work in the world. Before the Crusades she was the champion of Christendom in the Orient against the infidels, and by her military prowess, she saved Europe again and again. Face to face with barbarism, she was the center of a wonderful civilization — the most fastidious, the most refined that the Middle Ages knew in many years.

She was the teacher of the Slav and Asiatic Orient, whose peoples owe to her their religion, their literary language, their art, and their government; her all-powerful influence extended even to the West, which received from her immeasurable intellectual and artistic gifts. From her all the peoples who to-day inhabit Eastern Europe descend; and modern Greece especially owes much more to Christian Byzantium than to the Athens of Pericles and Phidias.

It is because of all this, because of what she did in the past, no less than by what she bequeathed to the future, that Byzantium still deserves attention and interest. However far away her history may seem, however inade-

quately known it may be to many people, it is not a dead history, deserving to be forgotten. Well did Ducange know it, when, in the middle of the seventeenth century, by his editions of the Byzantine historians, by the learned commentaries with which he accompanied them, by a number of admirable books, he laid the foundation for the scientific history of Byzantium, and opened broad and luminous vistas in this still unexplored domain. In the country of Ducange during the last fifty years, the tradition of the studies of which he was the founder has been revived; and without decrying what has been done elsewhere, in Russia and Greece, in England and Germany, it may perhaps be permissible to say that, if the delvers into Byzantine history have earned the freedom of the city in the scientific world, it is chiefly to France that they owe it.

I have been asked with polite insistence to write a book which we still lack — a brief, condensed manual of Byzantine history. This seemed to me by no means a useless task. Recently I have attempted in another volume, which has just been published, to draw a synthetic picture of what Byzantium was, to explain the deep-seated causes of her greatness and her decline, and to point out the eminent services which her civilization rendered to the world.[1]

This little book will give the reader a more analytical account of the thousand-year history of the Byzantine Empire. I have endeavored to bring out the most important ideas which control the evolution of this history; to present the essential facts, not so much restricting myself to a minute chronological detail, as grouping them by

1 Ch. Diehl; *Byzance, Grandeur et Décadence* (in the Bibliothèque de philosophie scientifique, dirigée par le Dr. G. Le Bon). Flammarion, 1919.

PREFACE

somewhat long periods, which will be more comprehensive, and will make clearer the significance and scope of the events narrated.

The tables at the end of the volume will make it easy for the reader to follow the chronological order of the most important events. But it has seemed to me that my book would be more useful to all who desire to have general knowledge of this vanished world, if, without omitting any of the necessary precision in details, I should trace the main outlines, the characteristic features, and the controlling ideas of the history of Byzantine civilization.

I wish to thank Hachette, who has authorized me to borrow from Scrader's "Atlas de géographie historique" two of the four maps which accompany this book. The illustrations, which will give some idea of Byzantine life and costume, and of the monuments of art which Byzantium produced, are taken from my "Manuel d'art byzantine" (Picard, 1910).

At the end of the volume there is a brief bibliography of the principal works for reading or reference.

Сн. D.

CONTENTS

CHAPTER I   page 3
The founding of Constantinople and the Beginnings of the Roman Empire in
the East, 330-518

CHAPTER II   17
The Reign of Justinian, and the Greek Empire in the Sixth Century, 518-610

CHAPTER III   40
The Dynasty of Heraclius.—The Arab Peril and the Transformation of the
Empire in the Seventh Century, 610-717

CHAPTER IV   53
The Isaurian Emperors and the Iconoclastic Controversy, 717-867

CHAPTER V   72
The Apogee of the Empire under the Macedonian Dynasty, 867-1081

CHAPTER VI   111
The Comnenus Dynasty, 1081-1204

CHAPTER VII   138
The Latin Empire of Constantinople and the Greek Empire of Nicæa, 1204-
1261

CHAPTER VIII   151
The Byzantine Empire under the Palæologi, 1261-1453

APPENDIX I   177
The Byzantine Emperors

APPENDIX II   181
Chronological Table of the Most Important Events in Byzantine History

APPENDIX III   189
Condensed Bibliography of the Principal Works for Reading or Reference

INDEX   193

HISTORY OF
THE BYZANTINE
EMPIRE

CHAPTER I

The Founding of Constantinople and the Beginnings of the Roman Empire in the East, 330-518

I. THE FOUNDING OF CONSTANTINOPLE AND THE CHARACTERISTICS OF THE NEW EMPIRE

ON May 11, A.D. 330, on the shores of the Bosphorus, Constantine solemnly dedicated his new capital, Constantinople.

Why did the Emperor, turning his back upon ancient Rome, remove to the East the seat of the monarchy? Not only had Constantine no personal liking for the turbulent pagan city of the Cæsars, but he also, and not without good reason, considered it badly placed for meeting the new exigencies with which the Empire was confronted. The Gothic peril on the Danube, the Persian peril in Asia, were imminent; and though the powerful tribes of Illyricum offered admirable resources for defense, Rome was too far away to make use of them for that purpose. Diocletian had realized this, and he too had felt the attraction of the Orient. At all events, the Byzantine Empire came into being on the day when Constantine founded "New

Rome." By virtue of its geographical situation, where Europe joins Asia, and of the military and economic importance resulting therefrom, Constantinople was the natural center around which the Eastern world could most readily group itself. On the other hand, by virtue of the Grecian stamp which had been imprinted upon it from the very beginning, and especially by virtue of the character which Christianity imparted to it, the new capital differed fundamentally from the old, and symbolized accurately enough the aspirations and the new tendencies of the Eastern world.

Moreover, long before this, a new conception of the monarchy had been astir in the Roman Empire. The transformation came about at the beginning of the fourth century, through contact with the Near East. Constantine strove to make of the imperial power an absolute domination by divine right. He surrounded it with all the splendor of costume, of the crown, and the royal purple; with all the pompous ceremonial of etiquette, with all the magnificence of court and palace. Deeming himself the representative of God on earth, believing that in his intellect he was a reflection of the supreme intellect, he endeavored in all things to emphasize the sacred character of the sovereign, to separate him from the rest of mankind by the solemn forms with which he surrounded him; in a word, to make earthly royalty as it were an image of the divine royalty.

In like manner, in order to increase the prestige and power of the imperial office, he proposed that the monarchy should be clothed with executive power, strictly hierarchical in form, closely safeguarded, and with all authority concentrated in the hands of the emperor. And finally, by making Christianity a state religion, by multiplying immunities and privileges in its favor, by defending it against heresy, and by extending his protection to it under all circumstances, Constantine gave an altogether different character to the power of the Emperor. Seated among the bishops, "as if he were one of them"; posing as the accredited guardian of dogma and discipline; intervening in all affairs of the Church; legislating and giving judgment in its name, organizing and directing it, convoking and presiding over its councils; dictating the formulas of faith, Constantine—and all his successors after him, whether orthodox or Arians—regulated according to one uniform principle the relations of State and Church. This is what came to be called *Cæsaropapism*, the despotic authority of the emperor over the Church; and the Oriental clergy, creatures of the court, ambitious and worldly, docile and pliant, accepted this tyranny without protest.

All this derived its inspiration from the deeply rooted conception of power dear to Oriental monarchies, and because of all this, although the Roman Empire endured for another century,—until 476, —although the Roman tradition remained alive and powerful, even in the Orient, until the end of the sixth century, nevertheless the Oriental part of the monarchy was concentrated around the city of Constantine and became, so to speak, conscious of its own importance.

From the fourth century on, despite the apparent and theoretical maintenance of Roman unity, in reality the two halves of the Empire were separated more than once, and were governed by different emperors; and when, in 395, Theodosius the Great died, leaving to his two sons Arcadius and Honorius an inheritance divided into two empires, the separation, which had long been imminent, became definitive. Thenceforth there was a Roman Empire of the East.

II. THE CRISIS OF THE BARBARIAN INVASION

DURING the long period between 330 and 518, two serious crises, while shaking the Empire to its foundations, finally gave it its peculiar form. The first was the crisis of the barbarian invasion.

After the third century, on all its frontiers, on the Danube as well as on the Rhine, the barbarians of Germany made their way into Roman territory by a gradual process of infiltration. Some came as soldiers, in small parties, or settled there as agricultural laborers; others, in whole tribes, attracted by the security and prosperity of the monarchy, solicited grants of land, which the imperial government willingly gave them. The great migrations which were incessantly taking place in that unstable Germanic world hastened this onrush of the barbarians, and finally made it formidable. In the fifth century, the Western Empire gave way before their irruption; and at first sight one might think that Byzantium was no better able than Rome to withstand their formidable onset.

In 376, the Visigoths, fleeing before the Huns, had demanded from the Empire protection and lands. Two hundred thousand of them had settled south of the Danube, in Mœsia. They soon revolted; one emperor, Valens, was killed while attempting to stay them on the plains of Adrianople (378); it required all the adroit vigor of Theodosius to conquer them. But after his death, in 395, the danger reappeared. Alaric, King of the Visigoths, descended upon Macedonia; he ravaged Thessaly and central Greece, and forced his way into the Peloponnesus, the feeble Arcadius (395–408), all the troops of the East being then in the West, being powerless to stop him; and when Stilicho, summoned from the West to the succor of the Empire, had surrounded the Goths at Pholoe in Arcadia (396), he preferred to let them escape and to come to terms with their leader. From that time on, during several years, the Visigoths were all-powerful in the Empire of the East, deposing the ministers of Arcadius, imposing their will on the sovereign, ruling as masters in the capital, and convulsing the state by their revolts. But the ambition of Alaric led him again toward the West; in 402 he invaded Italy; he returned thither in 410, and captured Rome; and by the definite settlement of the Visigoths in Gaul and in Spain, the peril that threatened the Empire of the East was exorcised.

Thirty years later, the Huns entered on the scene. Attila, founder of a vast empire which reached from the Don to Pannonia, crossed the Danube in 441, took Viminacium, Singidunum, Sirmium, and Naissus, and threatened Constantinople. The Empire, being defenseless, was compelled to pay tribute to him. This notwithstanding, in 447 the Huns again appeared south of the Danube. Again they came to terms. But the peril was still great, and disaster seemed to be at hand, when, in 450, the Emperor Marcianus (450–457) bravely refused to pay tribute. Once more fortune smiled on the Empire of the East. Attila turned his arms to the West. He returned thence, beaten and enfeebled; and a short time afterward his death (453) disrupted the empire he had founded.

In the second half of the fifth century, the Ostrogoths, in their turn, entered into conflict with the Empire, which was obliged to take them into its service, to allot lands to them (462), and to heap honors and money upon their leaders. And so we find them, in 474, actually interfering in the internal affairs of the monarchy. It was Theodoric who, on the death of the Emperor Leo (457–474), assured the triumph of Zeno over the rival who was disputing the throne with him.

From that time on, the barbarians were more exacting than ever. In vain did the Emperor attempt to turn the chiefs against one another (479): Theodoric pillaged Macedonia, and threatened Thessalonica, always demanding more and more; obtaining in 484 the title of consul; threatening Constantinople in 487. But he too allowed himself to be tempted by the charms of Italy, where, since 476, the Western Empire had been falling into decay, and which Zeno shrewdly proposed to him to reconquer. Once more the danger was averted.

Thus the barbarian invasion had passed along the frontiers of the Eastern Empire, or had encroached upon it only temporarily; so that New Rome remained intact, made greater, as it were, by the catastrophe that had overwhelmed Ancient Rome, and, because of that catastrophe, forced still farther eastward.

FOUNDING OF CONSTANTINOPLE

III. THE RELIGIOUS CRISIS

WE can hardly understand today the importance in the fourth and fifth centuries of all the great heresies—Arianism, Nestorianism, Monophysitism—which so profoundly agitated the Church and the Empire of the East. We commonly think of them as mere quarrels of theologians, debating hotly in complicated discussions concerning finespun and trivial formulas. In reality, they had a different meaning and greater scope. More than once they were a cloak for political interests and controversies which were to have far-reaching results on the destinies of the Empire. They had, moreover, a decisive effect in establishing the connection between Church and State in the East, and in determining the relations between Byzantium and the West. For these reasons they deserve to be carefully studied.

The Council of Nicæa (325) had condemned Arianism and had proclaimed that Christ was of the same essence as God. But the partisans of Arius did not yield under the anathema, and the fourth century was filled with a heated controversy—in which the emperors zealously took part—between the adversaries and defenders of orthodoxy. Arianism, conquering with Constantius at the Council of Rimini (359), was crushed by Theodosius at the Council of Constantinople (381); and from that moment was manifest the contrast between the Greek spirit, enamoured of metaphysical subtleties, and the candid genius of the Latin West; the incongruity between the Oriental episcopate, docile to the will of the prince, and the unyielding and haughty intransigence of the Roman pontiffs. The discussion that took place in the fifth century concerning the union of two natures—human and divine—in the person of Christ emphasized these differences still more, and agitated the Empire the more seriously because politics entered into the religious quarrel. In fact, at the same time that the popes in the West founded with Leo the Great (440–461) the pontifical monarchy, the patriarchs of Alexandria attempted in the East, with Cyril (412–444) and Dioscurus (444–451), to establish an Alexandrine papacy. And, in other matters, under cover of these disputes, the old national differences, and the separatist tendencies, which were still very much alive, found in the war against orthodoxy a propitious opportunity for showing their heads; and thus political interests and aims were closely intermingled with the religious conflict.

In 428, Theodosius II (408–450) had been reigning for twenty years at Byzantium, under the guardianship of his sister Pulcheria. Always a child, he passed his time in painting, and in illuminating or copying manuscripts; hence his nickname, "the Calligrapher." If his memory still lives in history, it is because he built the strong girdle of ramparts which for so many centuries protected Constantinople; and because, in the Theodosian Code, he caused to be brought together the imperial constitutions promulgated since Constantine. But, such as he was, he was destined to show extraordinary weakness and helplessness when confronted by the quarrels within the Church.

Nestorius, Patriarch of Constantinople, taught that

in Christ it was necessary to separate the divine and human personalities—that Jesus was only a man become God; and consequently he refused to the Virgin the appellation of *Theotokos* (mother of God). Cyril of Alexandria eagerly seized this opportunity to belittle the bishop of the capital, and, supported by the Papacy, he caused Nestorianism to be solemnly condemned at the Council of Ephesus (431); after which, imposing his will upon the Emperor, he reigned supreme over the Eastern Church. When Eutyches, several years later, amplifying the doctrine of Cyril, caused the nature of man to disappear more and more completely in the divine nature (this was Monophysitism), he found at hand, to defend him, the support of Dioscurus, Patriarch of Alexandria; and the council known as the "Robber Council of Ephesus" (449) seemed to assure the triumph of the Church of Alexandria.

The Empire and the Papacy, being equally alarmed, joined forces against these growing ambitions. The Council of Chalcedon (451), in conformity with the formula of Leo the Great, established the orthodox doctrine in regard to the union of the two natures, and accomplished at one and the same time the ruin of the Alexandrian dream, and the triumph of the State, which dominated the Council, and established more firmly than ever its authority over the Eastern Church.

But the Monophysites, although condemned, did not give way before their condemnation. They continued for a long time to establish churches with separatist tendencies in Egypt and Syria—a grave menace to the cohesion and unity of the monarchy. Rome, too, notwithstanding her victory in the field of dogma, had to accept, trembling with rage, the extension of the power of the Patriarch of Constantinople, who became, under the guardianship of the Emperor, the real pope of the Orient. Herein lay the germ of grave conflicts. In defiance of the Papacy, which was omnipotent in the West, the Eastern Church, hoping to free itself from the imperial domination, became a State Church, submissive to the will of the prince; and by her use of the Greek language; by her mystical tendencies, at odds with the theology of Rome, and by her ancient grudges against Rome, she tended more and more to establish herself as an independent organism. And thereby, again, the Roman Empire in the East took on an aspect peculiar to itself. The great councils were held in the East; the great heresies were born there; and, finally, the Church of the East, proud in the renown of its great doctors,—Saint Basil, Gregory of Nyssa, Gregory of Nazianzus, and John Chrysostom,—convinced of her intellectual superiority over the West, tended more and more toward separation from Rome.

IV. THE ROMAN EMPIRE OF THE EAST AT THE END OF THE FIFTH AND THE BEGINNING OF THE SIXTH CENTURY

THUS, about the time of the emperors Zeno (474–491) and Anastasius (491–518), arose the idea of a purely Oriental monarchy.

After the downfall of the Western Empire in 476, the Eastern remained the only Roman empire. Although it retained, for this reason, great prestige in the eyes of the barbarian sovereigns who had carved out for themselves kingdoms in Gaul, in Spain, in Africa, and in Italy; although it still claimed vague rights of suzerainty over them, yet in reality, by virtue of the territories that it actually possessed, this Empire was, above all, Oriental. It included the whole Balkan Peninsula, with the exception of the northwestern portions; Asia Minor as far as the mountains of Armenia; Syria as far as the Euphrates; Egypt; and Cyrenaica. These countries formed sixty-four provinces or *eparchies*, divided between two prefectures of the prætorium — that of the East (dioceses of Thrace, Asia, Pontus, the Orient, and Egypt), and that of Illyricum (diocese of Macedonia).

Although the government of the Empire was still administered on the Roman model, and based on the separation of the civil and military functions, the imperial power became more and more absolute, after the fashion of Oriental monarchies; and from 450 on, the ceremonial of consecration gave to it, in addition, the prestige of sacred unction and of divine investiture. The intelligent solicitude of the Emperor Anastasius assured to this empire well-defended frontiers, sound finances, and a more honest administration. And the political acumen of the sovereigns strove to restore moral unity in the monarchy by endeavoring, even at the cost of a rupture with Rome, to bring back the dissenting Monophysites. This was the object of the edict of union (Henotikon) promulgated in 482 by Zeno, the first effect of which was a schism between Byzantium and Rome. For more than thirty years

(484–518), with embittered intolerance, the popes and the emperors—especially Anastatius, a convinced and impassioned Monophysite—waged war; and during these disorders the Eastern Church succeeded in making herself into a separate body.

Meanwhile, the civilization of the Empire took on more and more an Oriental coloring. Even under the domination of Rome, Hellenism had remained vigorous and strong throughout the Greek Orient. Large and flourishing cities—Alexandria, Antioch, Ephesus —were the centres of a remarkable intellectual and artistic culture. Within their sphere of influence, in Egypt, in Syria, in Asia Minor, a civilization had sprung up which was thoroughly impregnated with the traditions of classical Greece. Constantinople, enriched by its founder with the masterpieces of Greece, and thus transformed into the most wonderful of museums, cherished no less enthusiastically the memories of Hellenic antiquity. Moreover, the Oriental world had been awakened by its contact with Persia, and had become conscious anew of its ancient traditions; in Egypt, in Syria, in Mesopotamia, in Asia Minor, the old traditional background reappeared, and the Oriental spirit reacted upon the countries previously Hellenized. Because of its hatred of pagan Greece, Christianity encouraged these national tendencies. And from the blending of these rival traditions a strong and fruitful activity sprang to life throughout the East.

Economically, intellectually, and artistically Syria, Egypt, and Anatolia assumed special importance during the fourth and fifth centuries: there Christian art, slowly, by a succession of scholarly efforts and investigations, prepared the way for its superb culmination in the masterpieces of the sixth century; and from that time on, it appeared as an essentially Oriental art. But while the old indigenous traditions and the never-forgotten separatist inclination were thus renewed in the provinces, Constantinople foreshadowed her future rôle by receiving and combining the different elements which diverse civilizations brought to her, by coördinating the rival intellectual tendencies and the differing artistic processes and methods in such wise as to produce a civilization of her own.

Thus the evolution which drew Byzantium toward the Orient seemed to be accomplished; and one could well believe that the dream was near realization, of a purely Oriental empire, despotically governed, well administered, strongly defended, renouncing all political connection with the West, to fall back upon herself, and not hesitating to break with Rome in order to reëstablish religious unity in the East, and to set up, under the protection of the State, a church almost independent of the papacy.

Unfortunately for the fulfilment of this dream, this Empire, at the end of the fifth and the beginning of the sixth century, was faced by a formidable crisis. After 502, the Persians had renewed the war in the East; in Europe, the Slavs and Bulgarians were beginning their incursions south of the Danube. In the interior, affairs were in extreme confusion. The capital was convulsed by the quarrels of the circus factions — the Greens and the Blues; the provinces, discontented, ruined by the war, crushed by taxes, grasped every occasion to put forward their national demands; the government was unpopular; a powerful orthodox opposition fought against its policies and furnished a plausible pretext for the revolts of the ambitious, of which the most serious was that of Vitalianus, in 514; finally, the persistent memory of the Roman tradition, keeping alive the idea of the necessary unity of the Roman world,—of "Romania,"—turned men's minds incessantly toward the West. To emerge from this unstable condition, there was need of a strong hand, a well-defined policy, with precise and steadfast aims. The reign of Justinian was to supply this need.

CHAPTER II

The Reign of Justinian, and the Greek Empire in the Sixth Century, 518 - 610

I. THE ACCESSION OF THE JUSTINIAN DYNASTY

IN 518, at the death of Anastatius, an obscure intrigue placed upon the throne Justin, commander-in-chief of the imperial guard. He was a Macedonian peasant, who had come to Constantinople some fifty years before, to seek his fortune; a brave soldier, but quite illiterate and without any experience in affairs of state. This upstart, then, who, at the age of almost seventy years, was destined to become the founder of a dynasty, would have been greatly embarrassed in the position of authority to which he was raised, had he not had by his side his nephew, Justinian, to advise him.

Justinian, who was, like Justin, a native of Macedonia,—the romantic tradition which makes of him a Slav is of much later date, and has no historical value, —had come early in life to Constantinople at the summons of his uncle, and had received there an education wholly Roman and Christian. He had experience in affairs, a ripe judgment, a well-developed character —everything that he required to be the coadjutor of the new sovereign. And, in fact, it was he who, from 518 to 527, governed in the name of Justin, pending the time when he himself should reign—from 527 to 565. Thus for nearly half a century Justinian guided the destinies of the Roman Empire of the East; and he stamped upon the epoch dominated by his powerful figure so deep an imprint, that his will alone sufficed to arrest the natural evolution which was carrying the Empire farther toward the Orient.

Under his influence, a new political orientation was apparent from the beginning of Justin's reign. The first thought of the government of Constantinople was to be reconciled with Rome, to put an end to the schism; and, in order to seal the alliance and to give to the Pope pledges of his orthodox zeal, Justinian for three years (518–521) savagely persecuted the Monophysites throughout the East. The new dynasty was strengthened by this reconciliation with Rome. Moreover, Justinian was shrewd enough to take, very cleverly, the measures necessary to assure the strength of the government. He rid it of Vitalianus, its most redoubtable adversary. Above all, he made it popular by a great show of largess and pomp.

But, thenceforth, Justinian had wider visions: he fully realized the importance to his ambition of the reëstablishment of peace with the papacy. For this reason, when Pope John I visited Constantinople in 525—the first of the Roman pontiffs to visit "New Rome"—Justinian arranged a triumphant reception for him in the capital. He knew how much such an attitude would gratify the West, and what comparisons would inevitably be drawn between the pious em-

perors who ruled in Constantinople and the barbarous
Arian monarchs who held sway in Africa and Italy.
And thus he paved the way for the great designs that
he was destined to achieve when, in 527, the death of
Justin gave him full power.

II. JUSTINIAN'S CHARACTER, HIS POLICY
AND HIS ENVIRONMENT

JUSTINIAN resembled in no way his predecessors, the
princes of the fifth century. This upstart elevated to
the throne of the Cæsars chose to be a Roman emperor, and he was in truth the last of the great emperors of Rome. Nevertheless, despite his indisputable
power of application and love of work,—one of his
courtiers called him "the Emperor who never sleeps,"
— despite a genuine and sincere desire for an orderly
and wise administration, Justinian, by reason of his
sombre and jealous despotism, his childish vanity, his
pugnacious activity, and because he was often irreso-
lute and weak in enforcing his will, would have seemed
to be, on the whole, rather a mediocre and ill-bal-
anced person, had it not been for his greatness of
mind. This Macedonian peasant was the eminent representative of two great ideas—the imperial idea and
the Christian idea; and because he represented those
ideas, his name will endure forever.

His mind full of the memories of Roman grandeur,
Justinian dreamed of reconstituting the Roman Empire as it was of old, of restoring the incontestable
rights of Byzantium, as heir of Rome, over the barbarous kingdoms of the West, of reëstablishing the

unity of the Roman dominions. Heir of the Cæsars, like them he was resolved to be the living law, the fullest incarnation of absolute power, and also the impeccable law-giver, the reformer, intent upon maintaining good order in the realm. Lastly, in his pride in his imperial rank, he chose to bedeck it with all conceivable pomp and magnificence. By the splendor of his buildings; by the luxury of his court; by the somewhat childish manner in which he called the fortresses that he rebuilt, "Justinians," after his own name; by the cities he restored; by the system of magistracies he established, he aimed to immortalize the glory of his reign, and to make his subjects feel, as he said, their incomparable good fortune in having been born in his time.

And he had other visions. The elect of God, his representative and vicar upon earth, he took it upon himself to be the champion of orthodoxy, whether in the wars that he undertook, whose religious character is incontestable, in the great effort that he made to propagate the orthodox faith throughout the world, or in the fashion in which he governed the Church and combatted heresy. All his life he pursued the realization of this two-fold dream, at once magnificent and ambitious; and to aid him, he had the good fortune to find capable ministers, such as the jurisconsult Tribonian, and the prefect of the prætorium, John of Cappadocia; good generals like Belisarius and Narses; and, above all, an admirable adviser in "the most revered wife whom God had given him," in her whom he took delight in calling "his sweetest charmer," the Empress Theodora.

Theodora also was of humble birth. Daughter of a bear-keeper in the Hippodrome, she had, if we are to believe the gossip of Procopius in his *Secret History*, scandalized her contemporaries by her life as a fashionable actress and by the notoriety of her adventures; and even more when she won the heart of Justinian, succeeded in inducing him to marry her, and ascended the throne with him. It is certain that, as long as she lived—she died in 548—she exercised an all-powerful influence over the Emperor, and governed the Empire as much as, and perhaps more than, he. The fact is that, despite her shortcomings—she loved money and power, and, in order to preserve the throne, she was often deceitful, cruel, and implacable in her hatreds—this great ambitious woman had some excellent qualities: energy, determination, a strong and resolute will, and a shrewd and far-seeing political genius; and it may be that she had a clearer vision than her imperial spouse. While Justinian dreamed of reconquering the West, of propping the rehabilitated Roman Empire on an alliance with the Papacy, she, like the true Oriental that she was, turned her eyes toward the East, with a more exact appreciation of the realities and necessities of the situation. She would have mitigated the religious dissensions which were inimical to the peace and power of the Empire, would have conciliated the dissident countries, like Syria and Egypt, by opportune concessions and greater tolerance, and, even at the cost of a break with Rome, would have restored the powerful unity of the Eastern monarchy. And we may well wonder whether the empire of which she dreamed, more compact, more homogeneous, and stronger, might not have resisted better the attacks of the Persians and the Arabs. At all events, her hand was felt everywhere—in the government, in diplomacy, in the religious policy; and even to-day, in the Church of San Vitale at Ravenna, in the mosaics that embellish the apse, her image, in all the splendor of sovereign majesty, faces Justinian's as an equal.

III. JUSTINIAN'S FOREIGN POLICY

AT the time of Justinian's accession the Empire had not recovered from the grave crisis through which it had been passing since the end of the fifth century. During the last months of Justin's reign, the Persians, aggrieved by the encroachments of the imperial policy in the Caucasus, in Armenia, and on the frontiers of Syria, had renewed the war; and thus the better part of the Byzantine army was immobilized in the East. In the interior, the feuds between the Greens and Blues fostered a dangerous political agitation, which was aggravated by the deplorable corruption of the government and the resulting discontent. It was most essential for Justinian to do away with these embarrassments, which delayed the execution of his ambitious designs upon the West. Not seeing, or not choosing to see, the extent of the Eastern peril, he signed with the Great King[1] the treaty of 532, which cost him large concessions, but left him entirely free to dispose of his military forces. On the other hand, he took stern measures to repress civil commotion when the formidable uprising of January 532, which has always

---

[1] Khusrau I, 531-579. The name is variously spelled Khosru and Chosroes.

been called *Nika*, from the rallying cry of the insurgents, filled Constantinople with conflagrations and blood during a whole week. In those days of revolution, when the throne was near foundering, Justinian owed his salvation to the courage of Theodora and the energy of Belisarius. But the brutality of the suppression, which strewed the floor of the Hippodrome with 30,000 corpses, resulted in establishing order in the capital for a long time, and in making the Emperor's power more absolute than ever. In 532, Justinian's hands were freed.

The Rehabilitation of Imperial Authority in the West.— Conditions in the West favored his projects. In Africa, as in Italy, the tribes, being governed by heretical barbarian rulers, loudly demanded the restoration of the imperial authority; and the prestige of the Empire was so great that even the Vandal and Ostrogothic kings acknowledged the legitimacy of the Byzantine claims. Moreover, the rapid decadence of those barbaric kingdoms left them powerless against the attacks of Justinian, and their dissensions prevented them from making common cause against the common enemy. When, therefore, in 531, the usurpation of Gelimer offered Byzantine diplomacy a pretext for intervening in Africa, Justinian, placing his trust in the formidable instrument of war which he had at hand in his excellent army, did not hesitate, being desirous to free the African Catholics from the "Arian captivity," and to make the Vandal kingdom once more a part of the imperial whole. In 533, Belisarius embarked at Constantinople with an army of 10,000 infantry and from 5000 to 6000 cavalry. The campaign was as short as it was successful. Defeated at Decimum and Tricamarum, Gelimer, surrounded in his retreat from Mount Pappua, was obliged to surrender (534). Within a few months, some regiments of cavalry—for it was the cavalry that played the decisive rôle, contrary to all expectation—entirely destroyed the kingdom of Genseric. The victorious Belisarius received the honors of a triumph at Constantinople. Although it took fifteen years more, from 534 to 548, to put down the revolts of the Berbers and the uprisings of the mercenary and undisciplined troops of the Empire, yet Justinian could fairly boast of having reconquered the larger part of Africa, and could proudly assume the surnames of Vandalicus and Africanus.

The Ostrogoths in Italy looked on without raising a hand at the subjugation of the Vandal kingdom. Before long, their own turn came. The assassination of Amalasuntha, daughter of Theodoric the Great, by her husband Theodahad (534) gave Justinian a pretext for interfering; but this time the war was harder to win, and longer. Belisarius succeeded in conquering Sicily (535), in taking Naples, and then Rome, where he withstood for a whole year (March, 537, to March, 538) a memorable siege by the army of the new King of the Ostrogoths, Vitiges. Later, he took Ravenna (540), and led Vitiges as a captive to the feet of the Emperor. But the Goths rallied under the leadership of the shrewd and energetic Totila. Belisarius, being sent again into Italy with very inadequate forces, failed there lamentably (544–548). It required the vigorous leadership of Narses to crush the resistance of the Ostrogoths at Taginæ (552), to beat down the last opposition of the barbarians in Campania (553), and to rid the peninsula of the Frankish hordes of Leutharis and Bucelin (554). It had taken twenty years to reconquer Italy. Again Justinian's optimism had led him to believe too soon that the conquest was complete; and perhaps, too, he postponed too long the great effort necessary to break the power of the Ostrogoths at a single blow. It was with altogether inadequate forces—scarcely 25,000 or 30,000 troops—that he undertook to bring Italy back under the imperial authority; and in consequence the war dragged along deplorably.

In Spain also Justinian took advantage of favorable circumstances to interfere in the dynastic quarrels of the Visigothic kingdom (544) and to reconquer the southeastern part of the country.

Thanks to his fortunate campaigns, Justinian could flatter himself that his dream had come true. Thanks to his persevering ambition, Dalmatia, Italy, all of eastern Africa, southern Spain, and the islands of the western Mediterranean—Sicily, Corsica, Sardinia, and the Baleares—had returned to the Roman fold: the Empire was almost doubled in extent of territory. By the occupation of Septem (Ceuta) the authority of the Emperor reached as far as the Pillars of Hercules; and if we except the parts of the coast still held by the Visigoths in Spain and Septimania,[1] and by the Franks in Provence, the Mediterranean was once more a Roman sea. It is true that neither Africa nor Italy re-

[1] In Southern France.

entered the imperial domain in all its former extent, and they were exhausted and ravaged by so many years of war.

But these conquests gave an unquestionable impetus to the prestige and glory of the Empire; and Justinian spared no effort to solidify it. Reconquered Africa and Italy formed as before two prefectures, and the Emperor strove to exhibit the Empire to the various peoples in the exact form in which it had formerly been familiar to them. Reparatory measures partially effaced the disasters of the war. Defensive precautions —the creation of great military bodies; the delimitation of boundaries (*limites*), which were held by special troops, the soldiers of the frontier (*limitanei*); the construction of a powerful network of fortresses— guaranteed the security of the country. Justinian might well flatter himself that he had restored in the West that perfect peace, that "perfect order," which was in his eyes the symbol of a truly civilized state.

The Wars in the East.—Unfortunately, these great undertakings had sapped the strength of the Empire, and had caused it to neglect the East; and the East took its revenge in most formidable fashion.

The first war with Persia (527–532) was only a forerunner of the peril that was impending. As neither of the two adversaries chose to go all lengths, the struggle was indecisive: the victory of Belisarius at Dara (530) was offset by his defeat at Callinicum (531), and both sides made haste to conclude a halting peace (532). But the new King of Persia, Khusrau Nushirvan (531–579), being active and ambitious, was not

the man to be content with these results. Seeing that
Byzantium had her hands full in the West, and, above
all, being ill at ease as to the projects of universal
domination of which Justinian made no secret, he descended upon Syria in 540, and pillaged Antioch; in
541, he invaded the country of the Lazi, and took
Petra; in 542, he devastated Commagene; in 543, he
defeated the Greeks in Armenia; in 544, he laid waste
Mesopotamia. Even Belisarius was powerless to conquer him. It was necessary to conclude a truce (545),
which was renewed several times, and, in 562, to sign
a fifty-years' treaty, whereby Justinian bound himself to pay tribute to the Great King, and forbade all
religious propaganda in Persian territory. Although at
this price, he retained the country of the Lazi, the ancient Colchis, nevertheless the Persian menace, after
this long and disastrous war, was no less to be dreaded
in the future.

Meanwhile, in Europe, the frontier of the Danube
gave way before the attacks of the Huns, who in 540
carried fire and the sword into Thrace, Illyricum, and
Greece as far as the Isthmus of Corinth, and forced
their way even to the neighborhood of Constantinople; of the Slavs, who devastated Illyricum in 547
and 551, and in 552 threatened Thessalonica; of the
Huns again in 559, when they appeared before the
capital, which was saved with great difficulty by the
bravery of old Belisarius. In addition, other barbarians, the Avars, appeared upon the scene, insolent and
menacing. To be sure, none of these invasions resulted in the permanent settlement of a foreign people
within the Empire; but the Balkan Peninsula was,

none the less, terribly ravaged. The Empire paid dearly in the East for Justinian's triumphs in the West.

Defensive Measures and Diplomacy.—Justinian, meanwhile, in the East as in the West, endeavored to ensure the defense and security of the imperial domain. By the institution of high military commands entrusted to the *magistri militum;* by the creation on all the frontiers of military boundaries (*limites*), occupied by special troops (*limitanei*), he reconstructed, in face of the barbarians, what was formerly called the "bulwark of the Empire" (*prætentura imperii*). But, most important of all, he built along all the frontiers a continuous line of fortresses, which covered all the strategic points and formed several successive barriers against invasion; behind these, for greater security, the whole territory was covered with strongholds. Even to this day we find in many places the imposing ruins of these citadels, which were erected by hundreds in all the provinces of the Empire; and they bear eloquent witness to the greatness of the effort by which, according to Procopius, Justinian veritably "saved the monarchy."

Lastly, Byzantine diplomacy, supplementing the military measures, did its utmost to ensure the prestige and influence of the Empire throughout the whole world. By a judicious distribution of favors and money, by ingenious craft in inciting the enemies of the Empire against one another, it brought under the suzerainty of Byzantium the barbarian tribes that drifted along the frontiers of the monarchy, and made them harmless. By religious propaganda, too, it brought them within the Byzantine sphere of influence. The missions that carried Christianity from the shores of the Black Sea to the plains of Abyssinia, and to the oases of the Sahara, were one of the most characteristic features of Grecian policy in the Middle Ages.

Thus the Empire established for itself a constituency of vassals: Arabs, from Syria and Yemen, Berbers from North Africa, Lazi and Tzani from the farthest confines of Armenia, Heruli, Gepidæ, Lombards, Huns on the Danube, even the Frankish sovereigns in far-distant Gaul, where they prayed in the churches for the Roman Emperor. Constantinople, where Justinian received the barbarian sovereigns in magnificent fashion, seemed the capital of the universe. And although it is true that, during the last years of his reign, the aged Emperor allowed the military system to become disorganized, and took over-much pleasure in practising a disastrous sort of diplomacy, which, by distributing money among the barbarians, dangerously aroused their cupidity, on the other hand, it is certain that, so long as the Empire was strong enough to defend itself, his diplomacy, supported by military force, seemed to his contemporaries a marvel of prudence, wisdom, and good sense ($\epsilon \dot{v} \beta o v \lambda \acute{\iota} a$). Despite the heavy sacrifices which the formidable ambition of Justinian cost the Empire, even his detractors have admitted that "the natural rôle of a high-minded emperor is to seek to aggrandize his empire and add to its renown."[1]

[1]Procopius.

IV. THE INTERNAL GOVERNMENT OF JUSTINIAN

THE internal government of the Empire gave no less concern to Justinian than did the defense of its territory. Urgent administrative reforms forced themselves upon his attention. A dangerous religious crisis demanded his thoughtful care.

Legislative and Administrative Reform.—The Empire was in an extraordinarily disturbed condition. The government was venal and corrupt; disorder and destitution reigned in the provinces; the administration of justice, thanks to the obscurity of the law, was arbitrary and partial; and one of the most serious consequences of this condition was that the taxes came in very slowly. Justinian had too much taste for order, a too earnest desire for a centralized government, and too great solicitude for the public good, to tolerate such a state of affairs. Besides, he was in constant need of money for his great enterprises.

Therefore he undertook a twofold reform. In order to give to the Empire "definite and indisputable laws," he entrusted an important legislative task to his minister Tribonian. A commission, convoked in 528 to reform the Code, gathered together and classified in a single body of laws the principal imperial constitutions promulgated since the time of Hadrian. This was the Justinian Code, which was published in 529, and of which a new edition appeared in 534. Soon after came the *Digest*, or *Pandects*, in which another commission, appointed in 530, brought together and classified the decisions drawn from the works of the

great jurisconsults of the second and third centuries—
an enormous task, which was completed in 533. The
Institutes summarized in a single manual, for the use
of students, the principles of the new Code. Finally,
the collection of new ordinances (*Novellæ*), published
by Justinian between 534 and 565, completed the imposing monument known as the *Corpus Juris Civilis*.

Justinian was so proud of this great legislative work
that he forbade it to be touched in the future, or to be
modified by any commentary; and that he made it the
immutable basis of legal instruction in the schools of
law established at Constantinople, at Beirut, and at
Rome. And, in truth, despite certain defects; despite
the haste with which the work was done, entailing
repetitions and contradictions; despite the regrettable
fashion in which the noblest monuments of the Roman
law were torn in pieces, this was a very great work,
one of the most fruitful for the progress of mankind.
If the Justinian law provided the imperial power with
the foundation of its absolute authority, it also, in the
civilization of the Middle Ages, conserved, and, later,
taught again to the West, the idea of the State, and
the principles of social organization. Also, by perme-
ating the rigor of the old Roman law with the new
spirit of Christianity, it introduced into the law a regard, hitherto unknown, for social justice, public
morality, and humanity.

In order to reform the government and the administration of justice, Justinian, in 535, promulgated two
momentous decrees, outlining for all officials the new
duties that he laid upon them, and enjoining upon

them above all else a scrupulous honesty in the government of the subject. At the same time, the Emperor abolished the sale of offices, increased salaries, suppressed useless departments, and, to ensure better order in a whole category of provinces, united the civil and military powers there: a tentative reform which was destined to be fruitful of results in the administrative history of the Empire.

He reorganized the administration of justice and the civil service in the capital; he gave a great impetus to public works throughout the Empire, building roads, bridges, aqueducts, baths, theatres, and churches; and he rebuilt with incredible magnificence the city of Constantinople, which had been partially destroyed in the insurrection of 532. Lastly by a careful economic policy, Justinian applied himself to developing the industrial wealth and commercial activity of the Empire;[1] and according to his custom, he boasted of having, "by his brilliant ideas, given a new flower to the State."

As a matter of fact, however, despite the Emperor's excellent intentions, the administrative reform came to nothing. The heavy burden of expenditure and the constant need of money which resulted from it led to an atrocious fiscal tyranny, which reduced the Empire to destitution, and exhausted its resources. And from this great effort at reform only one thing resulted— the suppression, in 541, for reasons of economy, of the consular office.

[1] It was in the reign of Justinian, about 577, that two monks brought from China the secret of raising silkworms, which, by making possible the founding of the silk industry in Syria, partially freed Byzantium from its dependence upon imports from abroad.

The Religious Policy.—Like all the emperors who had followed one another on the throne since Constantine, Justinian gave much thought to the Church, for reasons of state no less than because of his zest for religious controversy. To show his pious zeal, he had bitterly opposed the heretics: in 529 he had ordered the closing of the University of Athens, where several pagan professors were leading an obscure existence, and he had vigorously persecuted dissenters. Moreover, he proposed to rule the Church as its master, and in exchange for his protection and for the favors he had heaped upon it, he despotically and brutally imposed his will upon it, proclaiming himself curtly, "emperor and priest."

However, more than once he was embarrassed as to what course he should pursue. For the success of his Western enterprises he needed to maintain the harmonious relations that he had reëstablished with the Papacy; to restore political and moral unity in the East, it was necessary for him to conciliate the Monophysites, who were still numerous and powerful in Egypt, Syria, Mesopotamia, and Armenia. Between Rome, which demanded the condemnation of the dissenters, and Theodora, who advised a return to the conciliatory policy of Zeno and Anastatius, the Emperor was more than once at a loss what to do; and his hesitating will labored to find, among many antagonisms, a common ground of understanding, in order to solve the dilemma.

First, to please Rome, he allowed the Council of Constantinople, in 536, to hurl anathema at the dissenters, persecuted them relentlessly (537–538), and

attacked their stronghold—Egypt; then, to please
Theodora, he allowed the Monophysites to reëstablish their church (543), and endeavored to obtain from
the Papacy, at the Council of Constantinople, in 553,
an ambiguous condemnation of the decisions of Chalcedon. This was the affair of the "Three Chapters,"[1]
which, for more than twenty years (543–565), convulsed the Empire, and provoked schism in the Western Church, without bringing peace to the Orient.
There was no useful result from all the outlay of se-
verity and arbitrariness which Justinian employed
against his adversaries, and of which the Pope Vigilius
was the most illustrious victim. The policy of union
and of tolerance which Theodora advised was, without doubt, wise and prudent; but Justinian's hesita-
tion in adopting a definite course of action had no
other effect, despite his good intentions, than a revival of the separatist tendencies of Egypt and Syria,
and an aggravation of their national hatred against
the Empire.

V. BYZANTINE CIVILIZATION IN THE SIXTH CENTURY

THE reign of Justinian is a decisive epoch in the history of Byzantine civilization. Writers of talent, historians like Procopius, Agathias, John of Ephesus,
and Evagrius, poets like Paul the Silentiary, theologians like Leontius of Byzantium, kept alive, not
without distinction, the traditions of classical Greek

---

[1] So called because the discussion concerned extracts from the works of three
theologians, Theodore of Mopsuestia, Theodoret of Cyrrhus, and Ibas of
Edessa, whose teaching had been approved by the Council of Chalcedon, and
had been condemned by Justinian, to please the Monophysites.

literature; and it was near the dawn of the sixth century that Romanos, "the prince of melody," created religious poetry, perhaps the most perfect and most original expression of Byzantine genius.

The splendor of the arts was still more remarkable. This was the time when the slow evolution that the local schools of art in the East had been passing through for two centuries reached its final development in Constantinople. And as Justinian had a taste for building, as he had the good fortune to find eminent artists to carry out his plans and was able to place unlimited resources at their disposal, the result was that the monuments of that period—marvels of skill, of audacity, and of magnificence—marked in definitive creations the apogee of Byzantine art.

Never has art appeared more varied, more fruitful, more free; all methods of construction, all types of buildings, were found there: basilicas like San Apollinare Nuovo at Ravenna and Saint Demetrius at Salonica; churches on the polygonal plan, like those of Saints Sergius and Bacchus at Constantinople, or San Vitale at Ravenna; cruciform buildings crowned by five cupolas, like the Church of the Holy Apostles; architectural works, of which Saint-Sophia—built between 532 and 537, by Anthemius of Tralles and Isidore of Miletus—is still, because of the originality of the plan, the lightness of structure, the skilful audacity of the arrangement, the cleverly managed balancing of the parts, and the rare harmony of the proportions, the unrivaled masterpiece.

In the interior of these edifices, the ingenious diversity of coloring of the marbles, the delicate carving of the sculptures, and the rich decoration of the mosaics on backgrounds of blue and gold, impart an incomparable magnificence, of which, even to-day, lacking the ruined mosaics of the Church of the Holy Apostles and those which are scarcely visible under the Turkish patching of Saint-Sophia, we can obtain some idea in the churches of Parenzo and Ravenna, and in what remains of the beautiful decorations of the Church of St. Demetrius at Salonica. Everywhere, in jewels, fabrics, ivories, and manuscripts, is manifest the same brilliant splendor and solemn majesty that marked the advent of the new style. Under the combined influences of the East and of ancient tradition, Byzantine art knew, in the time of Justinian, its first golden age.

VI. THE DISINTEGRATION OF JUSTINIAN'S WORK
(565–610)

IF we consider Justinian's reign as a whole, we cannot fail to realize its incomparable grandeur and the unequalled prestige that it momentarily gave to the monarchy. We may, however, wonder whether this grandeur was not more apparent than real, and whether this superb effort of imperialism, by arresting the natural evolution of the Eastern Empire, by draining its vigor in the interest of overweening ambition, did not, on the whole, do it more harm than good.

In all the enterprises of Justinian, there was always a dangerous disproportion between the end to be pursued and the resources available for attaining it; lack of money was the constant sore spot, which retarded the most magnificent projects, and foiled the most praiseworthy purposes. To remedy this, it was necessary to increase the exactions of the treasury to the point at which they became intolerable; and inasmuch as, in the last years of his reign, Justinian, in his old age, neglected everything more and more, the plight of the realm when he died, in 565, at the age of 87, was utterly deplorable. The Empire was exhausted both financially and militarily; on all the frontiers grave perils were rising above the horizon; in the interior, public authority was weakened, in the provinces by the development of a great feudal system of landholding, in the capital by the incessant feuds between Greens and Blues; people lived only from hand to mouth; there was great misery everywhere; and contemporaries asked themselves with stupefaction, whither the wealth of the Romans had vanished. A settlement was inevitable; it was difficult and disastrous. It was the work of Justinian's successors, his nephew Justin II (565–578), Tiberius (578–582), and Maurice (582–602).

They resolutely inaugurated a new policy. Turning away from the West, where, indeed, the invasion of the Lombards (568) had already wrested from the Empire the half of Italy, Justinian's successors confined themselves to organizing there a strong defensive, by the creation of the Exarchates of Africa and Ravenna. At this price, they were able to turn their attention toward the East, and to assume a haughtier attitude toward the enemies of the Empire. Thanks to the measures that they took for reorganizing the army, the Persian war, which broke out anew in 572, and lasted until 591, was ended by an advantageous treaty, by the terms of which Persian Armenia was ceded to Byzantium. And although in Europe the Huns and Slavs savagely ravaged the Balkan Peninsula, capturing the fortresses on the Danube, besieging Thessalonica, menacing Constantinople (591), and even beginning to make permanent settlements, a series of victories finally carried the war again beyond the frontiers, and led the Byzantine troops to the Theiss (601).

Unluckily the domestic crisis ruined everything. Justinian had strained to excess the machinery of absolute government; when he died, the aristocracy raised its head, the separatist tendencies of the provinces began to manifest themselves anew, and the factions of the circus to stir up sedition. And, as the government was powerless to reform the financial situation, the disaffection constantly increased, aggravated by the administrative disorganization and the mutinous demonstrations in the army.

The religious policy made the general dissatisfaction even more acute. After a brief trial of toleration, persecution was resorted to, to put down the dissenters; and although Maurice put an end to it, yet the inopportune conflict which he allowed to break out between the Patriarch of Constantinople, pretender to the title of Œcumenical, and Pope Gregory the Great, increased the ancient bitterness between the East and the West. Despite his genuinely high qualities, Maurice, because of his rigid economy, was extremely unpopular; and the relaxation of political

authority made easy the success of the military revolution, which placed Phocas on the throne (602).

The new prince, who was a common soldier, could
maintain order only by terror (602–610); thereby he
completed the downfall of the monarchy. Khusrau II,
posing as Maurice's avenger, renewed the war; the
Persians conquered Mesopotamia, Syria, and Asia
Minor. In 608, they were at Chalcedon, opposite
Constantinople. In the interior, revolts, conspiracies,
uprisings, succeeded one another; the whole Empire
cried out for a savior.

He came from Africa. In 610, Heraclius, son of the
Exarch of Carthage, overthrew Phocas and founded a
new dynasty. After nearly a half-century of agitation,
Byzantium again had a leader to guide her destinies.
But during that same half-century, Byzantium had
been progressively turning again toward the East.
The transformation to the oriental form, interrupted
by the long reign of Justinian, was now to quicken its
pace and be consummated.

CHAPTER III

The Dynasty of Heraclius.—The Arab Peril and the Transformation of the Empire in the Seventh Century, 610-717

THE seventh century was one of the darkest periods in Byzantine history. It was a time of grave uncertainty, a critical moment, when it seemed as if the very existence of the Empire was at stake. Without, formidable perils, first from the Persians, and soon after, the more terrible peril from the Arabs, assailed the exhausted monarchy. Within, a complete transformation took place, which gave to the Byzantine State and to the Byzantine world in general a new aspect. Up to that time, the monarchy, in spite of everything, had continued to be in all respects a Roman empire: Latin was still the official language, and the Roman tradition kept alive the titles and the forms that Rome had established. At the beginning of the eighth century, on the contrary, a really Byzantine Empire had come into being, all whose forces were concentrated about Constantinople, and which became more and more Oriental in character.

DYNASTY OF HERACLIUS

I. THE RECONSTRUCTION OF THE EMPIRE BY HERACLIUS

WHEN Heraclius (610–641) ascended the throne, the plight of the monarchy seemed almost desperate. Each year the Persians made greater progress: in 612, they took Antioch, Apamea, Cæsarea; in 614, Damascus; in 615, they occupied Jerusalem, whence they carried away the Holy Cross and the most famous relics of Christendom to Ctesiphon; in 617, they occupied Egypt, and advanced into Asia as far as Chalcedon. Meanwhile, the Avars appeared before Constantinople (619); the Lombards gained ground in Italy, and the Empire finally lost its possessions in Spain.

Disheartened by all these disasters, Heraclius thought for a moment of leaving Constantinople and transporting the seat of authority to Africa. One man revived his courage by his indomitable energy—the Patriarch Sergius, whose influence was very great in the whole policy of the reign. Impulsive and high-strung, capable of great enthusiasms, as well as liable to sudden fits of depression, filled with an ardent religious faith, and burning to avenge Christianity for the outrages of the Persians; a courageous soldier too, an excellent administrator, and a great general, Heraclius reasserted himself. The Patriarch placed at his disposal the treasures of the Church; he himself, with untiring diligence, reorganized the army. In 622 he was ready for the struggle. For six years, not allowing himself to be turned aside by anything, not even by the formidable attack which the united Persians and Avars launched against Constantinople (626), he fought the armies of the Great King, carrying the war into the enemies' territory—into Azerbaijan (623) and into Persian Armenia (625); victorious at Nineveh (627), victorious at the gates of Ctesiphon (628), and entering into legendary history as the first of the Crusaders. The death of Khusrau II (628), and the revolution that followed, finally forced upon the Persians a humiliating peace, by which they restored all their conquests, and especially the Holy Cross, which Heraclius carried back in triumph to Jerusalem (629).

After these great military successes, Heraclius endeavored, by his religious policy, to restore moral unity to the Empire and win back the Monophysites of Syria and Egypt; he strove, in concert with the Patriarch Sergius and Cyrus of Alexandria, to find a formula of conciliation which should bring dissenters back into the orthodox fold. From this sprang the Monothelite doctrine, which the Emperor defined in his exposition of faith known as the *Ecthesis* (638), and of which he devoted himself to obtaining the acceptance both by the Monophysites and by the Roman Church.

The Empire, thanks to these efforts, seemed to be rehabilitated: its prestige in the East was restored; its influence, by virtue of the conversion of the Croats and the Serbs, again made itself felt to the northwest of the Balkan Peninsula. But these brilliant seemings only partly concealed actual exhaustion. The condition of the finances was deplorable; the separatist tendencies, which had so materially aided the success of the Persians, were not exorcised. Within a few years the Arab invasion was to destroy all the results of the

victories of Heraclius, at the same time that his religious policy was cultivating the germ of long-continued
dissensions and grave conflicts.

II. THE ARAB PERIL

THE beginning of the seventh century was marked by
a momentous event—the birth of Islam. In twenty
years, through its extraordinary expansion, the new
religion conquered the greater part of the Eastern
world, and made its way, at the expense of Persia and
Byzantium, from the banks of the Oxus to the shores
of the Syrtis Major.

In 634, the armies of the Caliph Omar attacked
Syria. The Byzantine troops were beaten at Ajnadaïn
(634); Damascus fell into the hands of the Mussulmans (635); the disaster of Yermuk (636) determined
Heraclius to bid an eternal farewell to Syria. The
tribes, too, being hostile to the Greeks, made haste to
go over to the victor. Jerusalem capitulated in 637;
Antioch in 638. Then came the turn of Mesopotamia
(629), of Egypt, which Amru conquered in two years
(640–642), without encountering any great resistance;
and Heraclius, aged and ill, died in despair.

Under his successor, Constans II (642–668), the
Arabs continued their progress. Cyrenaica and Tripoli
fell into their hands (642–643); in 647, they invaded
Northern Africa for the first time. They ravaged Asia
Minor (651), and subjugated Armenia (653). Finally,
having built a fleet, they threatened the preponder-
ance which Byzantium had held hitherto in the eastern waters. They conquered Cyprus (649), pillaged

Rhodes (654), and in 655, on the coast of Lycia, they inflicted a memorable defeat upon the Greek fleet commanded by the Emperor in person. Constantinople itself was in danger, and Constans II, deeming the Orient lost, went westward to pass the last years of his life (663–668).

This furthered the designs of the Ommiad caliphs, who had reigned at Damascus since 660. From that time on, an Arab invasion ravaged Asia Minor every year. In 668 the Mussulmans penetrated as far as Chalcedon. At the same time, they assumed the offensive in the West, established themselves in Northern Africa, where they founded Kairwan (669), and threatened Sicily. Finally, in 673, they made a supreme effort: they attacked Constantinople.

But the new Emperor, Constantine IV (668–685), was an energetic prince. Fruitlessly the Arabs assailed the Byzantine capital by land and sea for five whole years (673–678): they did not succeed in taking it. The Grecian fleet, to which the recent discovery of *Greek fire* gave an incontestable superiority, forced the Mussulman squadrons to retreat, and inflicted a terrible defeat upon them in the bay of Syllæum.

On land, the armies of the Caliph were beaten in Asia. Moaviyah had to resign himself to sign a treaty (678). This was the first check for Islam. Constantine IV might well be proud of his work. The prestige of the Empire was so far restored that all its adversaries of the monarchy bent the knee before it; and, says the chronicler Theophanus, profound tranquillity reigned in East and West.

DYNASTY OF HERACLIUS

III. THE RELIGIOUS POLICY AND THE WEST

AT the same time the Emperor restored peace in the Church. The religious policy of Heraclius had had serious consequences. Monothelism had aroused keen disaffection in Africa and Italy, which had found vent in the uprisings of the exarchs of Carthage (646) and of Ravenna (650) against the imperial authority, in the growing discontent of the Italian peoples, and in the ardent opposition of the Roman pontiffs. To no purpose had Constans II endeavored to pacify men's minds by promulgating the edict called the *Type* (648); in vain had he caused Pope Martin I (653) to be arrested and condemned; in vain had he gone in person to the West. Rome had been obliged to submit; but by favor of these events the Lombards had made new conquests.

Constantine IV realized that a different policy was imperative. The loss of Egypt and Syria made it useless thenceforth to seek an agreement with the Monophysites. In restoring religious tranquillity by an understanding with Rome, the Emperor hoped at one and the same time to bind what was left of Italy more closely to the Empire, and to obtain leisure to devote himself entirely to the political and military affairs of the monarchy. Consequently the Œcumenical Council of Constantinople (680–681) had the task of restoring religious unity; and, in full accord with the Papacy, it condemned the Monothelite heresy, and reëstablished the orthodox faith.

These were important results. When Constantine IV died in 685, the Empire seemed to have emerged from the crisis in which it had been very near going to pieces. To be sure, it had emerged terribly curtailed; to be sure, its economic prosperity was seriously impaired by the loss of Egypt, whose grain was one of the chief resources of the Empire, of Syria, whose flourishing industries were one source of its wealth, and of those harbors — Alexandria, Gaza, Antioch, and Beirut—which were the centres of prodigious commercial activity. To be sure, another black cloud was rising above the horizon: since 679, the Bulgarians, having crossed the Danube, had settled between that river and the Balkans. But, on the whole, the monarchy had resisted the furious assaults of Islam; the defense of its territory had been ensured by great administrative reforms; and the Empire, more compact, more homogeneous, freed from the danger of Oriental separatism and from the dead weight of the West (it was to lose Africa in 698, as it had lost Spain and half of Italy), seemed a solidly established organism, capable of surviving in the new and wholly Oriental form that it had assumed in the course of the seventh century.

IV. THE TRANSFORMATION OF THE EMPIRE
IN THE SEVENTH CENTURY

A SUBSTANTIAL transformation had, in truth, taken place. First of all, an ethnographic transformation. In the devastated and depopulated Balkan Peninsula, new tribes had established themselves, little by little. In the northwest, Heraclius had been obliged to tolerate the settlement of the Croats and Serbs, on condition that they should be converted to Christianity, and should become vassals of the Empire. The Slavs had found their way into other districts. There were Slavic cantonments in Mœsia and Macedonia, and up to the gates of Thessalonica, which the barbarians had attacked at different times, but had failed to capture. There were Slavs in Thessaly, in Central Greece as far as the Peloponnesus, and in the islands of the Archipelago; and, if it is an exaggeration to believe, as Fallmerayer maintains, that there was a complete slavization of those regions, the fact remains that many foreign elements had come in, to mingle with the Hellenic peoples, and that these invaders caused much trouble to the emperors of the seventh century, who succeeded only with difficulty in subduing and assimilating them. In the northeastern part of the peninsula, the Bulgarians had, later, settled in a body; and as they came in contact with the Slavic tribes living in the country, they had gradually become *slavized*, and had founded a strong state. No doubt, serious dangers to the Empire resulted from all this; but there was also an advantage in this blending of races: the Empire was rejuvenated by this infusion of new blood.

About the same time a change in government of great importance had taken effect. In the reign of Justinian, the system of government set up by Rome in certain provinces had been modified by the union of civil and military powers in the same hands. After Justinian, this practice became general, the better to ensure the defense of the frontiers. It was with this end in view that Maurice, at the end of the sixth century, created the Exarchate of Africa for protection against the Berbers, and that of Ravenna against the Lombards. In the seventh century, similar measures were taken in the East against the Arab and Bulgarian perils. The successors of Heraclius set up governments called *themes*—so called from a word which originally meant an army corps, and was very soon applied to the territory occupied by the corps. In these districts, supreme authority was entrusted to a military chief, the *strategis*, under whom the civil administration continued, but in a subordinate position. Thus arose in Asia the *themes* of Armenia, Anatolia, and the Opsikion, and in Europe, that of Thrace. The maritime districts and islands were organized in the same way; they formed the *maritime theme*. At the end of the seventh century, instead of being divided into *eparchis*, as in the Roman period, the Empire comprised seven or eight *themes*, of considerable size. Carried to completion and made general by the emperors of the eighth century, the government by *themes* was destined to endure as long as the Empire, and it marks the evolution toward a military form of government which is the characteristic feature of all mediæval states.

But, above all, in the seventh century the Empire became Hellenized. In the reign of Heraclius, in 627, there appeared for the first time in the imperial proclamation, in place of the ancient Roman nomenclature, the Greek appelation, "Basileus faithful in God" ($\pi\iota\sigma\tau\grave{o}\varsigma$ $\acute{e}\nu$ $\theta\epsilon\hat{\omega}$ $\beta\alpha\sigma\iota\lambda\epsilon\acute{\nu}\varsigma$), which thenceforth was the style used by all the Byzantine emperors. At the same time, Greek became the official language. Justinian, in his day, although he still regarded Latin as the "national language" of the Empire, had condescended to promulgate most of his *Novellæ* in the "vernacular, which is Greek," to make them more intelligible. In the seventh century, all the imperial decrees and all the edicts of the government were drawn up in Greek. In the administration, the old Latin titles disappeared, or were Hellenized, and new ones took their place— *logothetes, eparchs, strategoi, drongaires.* In the army, where Asiatics and Armenians predominated, Greek became the language of command. And, although the Byzantine Empire continued, until its last day, to call itself the "Empire of the Romans," Latin was scarcely understood there, and the word ʹΡωμαῖοι meant Greeks. Finally, in place of the refined and slightly artificial language used by the writers of the fifth and sixth centuries, in which they continued the tradition of classical literature, vulgar Greek made its appearance, and became the spoken language of most of the peoples of the monarchy.

While the Empire was becoming Hellenized, the religious imprint with which it had always been stamped became more profound, because of the larger place that the Church filled in public life and in society. Religious questions held a position of essential importance in the State; the wars of Heraclius were so many crusades, and the emperors were passionately interested in theological problems. From that time, orthodoxy and nationality meant the same thing at Byzantium. Moreover, the Patriarch of Constantinople, who had now become the sole head of the Byzantine Church since the Arabs had conquered the patriarchates of Alexandria, Antioch, and Jerusalem, took on the aspect of a very great personage, whose influence in the government was often omnipotent.

No less significant facts are the development of monasticism, the great number and wealth of the convents, the influence which the monks exercised by their direction of men's consciences and the veneration which attached to their persons and to the sacred images which their monasteries possessed. Indeed, Paganism had disappeared since the end of the sixth century, and with it the spirit of antiquity; from the beginning of the seventh century Byzantine literature assumed a form that was almost entirely religious and popular; intellectually and artistically, this period was one of the least productive that Byzantium ever knew.

But, with all this, Greek, which was always the language of the Church in the East, completed its conquest of the Empire; and as the ambition of the patriarchs of Constantinople offended the susceptibilities of the Romans, the religious policy of the emperors, who antagonized and outraged the popes, and the increasing misunderstanding and hostility between the East and the West, paved the way for the rupture between those two hierarchies, and helped to drive the Byzantine Empire back toward the East. Thenceforth the monarchy had two powerful supports, which were to ensure its existence, and to give it its distinctive character for centuries to come—Hellenism and the orthodox faith.

DYNASTY OF HERACLIUS

V. THE END OF THE DYNASTY OF HERACLIUS AND THE DECADENCE OF THE EMPIRE (685–717)

A SINGLE vigorous hand would have sufficed to bring back prosperity to the Empire thus transformed. Unfortunately, the imprudence and follies of Justinian II (685–695) endangered all the results obtained by his father. War broke out anew with the Bulgarians (689) and the Slavs; it broke out anew with the Arabs, and ended in disaster (692). On the other hand, the religious policy brought on a rupture with Rome, and led to insurrections in Italy. In 695, a revolution overturned the dynasty of Heraclius and opened a period of twenty years of anarchy (695–717). Six emperors succeeded one another on the throne, following an equal number of *coups-d'état;* and by favor of these commotions Byzantine Africa fell definitively into the hands of the Mussulmans (693–698). In the East, despite the efforts and temporary successes of Tiberius III (698–705), the Arabs ravaged Asia Minor; invaded Armenia, which had revolted against Byzantium (703), and Cilicia (711); captured Amasia (712), and Antioch in Pisidia (713); devastated Galatia (714); besieged Amorium (716), and took Pergamum. Meanwhile, in Europe the Bulgarians, whose Khan, Terbel, had restored Justinian II to the throne in 705, invaded the Empire (708), and even appeared before Constantinople (712). The monarchy had its back to the wall.

The situation at home was scarcely better. A dangerous intellectual and moral debasement was manifest in the society of this period. During the civil wars a wave of savagery, of cruelty and treachery penetrated everywhere; incessant revolts, rampant ambitions, insurrections breaking out on all sides, in Italy as well as in the Chersonese, testify to a growing lack of faith and loyalty. Superstition made formidable progress: worship of relics, belief in the miraculous virtues of the sacred images, in the marvelous and the supernatural,—witness the rôle ascribed to the Virgin at the siege of Constantinople in 626, or the intervention attributed to St. Demetrius in the defense of Thessalonica,—the tendency to fatalism, had sovereign sway over men's minds in those days; and all that we know of the morals of ecclesiastics as well as of the laity bears witness to an extraordinary demoralization. The influence that the monks exercised and the agitation that they kept alive were another source of disorder. And because of all this, many people were profoundly perturbed and scandalized, and justly so.

The Empire was awaiting, was loudly demanding, a savior and a leader. He appeared in the person of Leo the Isaurian. When, in 717, the *strategos* of Anatolia, in concert with the *strategos* of Armenia, rose against the Emperor whom the troops of the Opsikion had proclaimed, and marched to Constantinople, everybody—the Senate and the people, the Patriarch and the soldiers—pronounced themselves in his favor. The Isaurian dynasty, which ascended to the throne with him, was to reëstablish order and security in the Empire, and gloriously to rehabilitate it.

CHAPTER IV

*The Isaurian Emperors and the Iconoclastic
Controversy*, 717-867

I. THE RECONSTRUCTION OF THE EMPIRE UNDER THE
FIRST TWO ISAURIAN EMPERORS (717-775)

THE new Emperor, Leo III (717-740), was a remarkable man. Being an excellent general, he
had tried, not without success, to defend Asia against
the Mussulmans; being a shrewd diplomat and good
organizer, he had all the qualities of a statesman. His
son, Constantine V (740-775), whom he early associated with himself in power, in order to ensure the
duration of the dynasty, was an able ruler, notwithstanding the accusations and slanders which his enemies heaped upon him, and notwithstanding the nick-
names, *copronymus* (an obscene epithet) and *caballi-
nos* (ostler), with which they delighted to revile him.
He was intelligent, energetic, a great warrior and a
great organizer; and although he was even more dicta-
torial, violent, harsh, and choleric than his father, it
is none the less true that the first two Isaurians were
very great emperors, whose glorious memory long remained dear to the army and the people of Byzantium, and to whom even their adversaries could not

refuse to do justice. The fathers at the Council of Nicæa, while criticizing severely the religious policy of Leo III and Constantine V, praised their bravery, the victories they won, the wise measures they took for the well-being of their subjects, the constitutions they promulgated, their civil institutions—in fact, everything that had earned for them the gratitude of the people. And, in very truth, the first two Isaurians were the glorious artificers of the reorganization of the Empire.

The Foreign Policy.—A few months after the accession of Leo III, the Arabs appeared before Constantinople and attacked it by land and sea; even the winter, which was very severe, did not interrupt the operations. But the Mussulman fleets were defeated in several battles; the land army, exhausted by famine, underwent a serious disaster. After a year of useless efforts (from August, 717, to August, 718), the Arabs raised the siege. For Leo III, it was a glorious beginning of his reign; for Islam, a great catastrophe; and an event of very different significance from the victory won fifteen years later (732) by Charles Martel, on the plains of Poitiers. The onrush of the Arabs was definitively arrested, and the pious Byzantines might justly be proud to see that God and the Virgin were still loyally protecting the Christian City and Empire.

Nevertheless, despite this disaster, the Arabs were still to be feared. After several years of respite, they resumed the offensive, and almost every year Asia Minor suffered from their invasions. But the defeat that the two emperors inflicted upon them at Akroi-

non (739) taught them a severe lesson. Constantine
V took advantage of it to assume the offensive in
Syria (745), to reconquer Cyprus (746), and to carry
the war to the Euphrates and into Armenia (751).
Also, the internal conflicts that convulsed the Arab
Empire—the accession to power of the Abbassides
(750), who transferred the capital of the Caliphs from
near-by Damascus to distant Bagdad—were singularly favorable to the successes of the Byzantines.
Throughout the reign of Constantine V, the war went
favorably for the Greeks; and after him, his son, Leo
IV, was able to invade Syria in 778, with an army of
100,000 men, and in 779 triumphantly to drive the
Mussulmans out of Asia Minor. The Arab peril, so
portentous in the seventh century, ceased to be a
menace to the Empire.

Constantine V endeavored, at the same time, to
avert the Bulgarian peril. In 755 he took the offensive, and in nine successive campaigns inflicted such
sanguinary defeats upon the barbarians, at Marcellæ
(759) and Anchialus (762), that in 764, panic-stricken,
they did not even attempt further resistance, and con-
sented to make peace. The war that began again in
772, and lasted to the end of the reign, was no less
successful; and even if Constantine V did not succeed
in destroying the Bulgarian state, he did, at least, restore the prestige of the Byzantine arms in the Balkan
Peninsula. In addition, he suppressed the uprisings of
the Slavs in Thrace and Macedonia (758), and, following the example of Justinian II, he settled some of
their tribes in Asia Minor, in the *theme* of Opsikion
(762).

Internal Reform.—While they were imposing respect for the Empire upon its enemies, the two Isaurian emperors applied themselves to strengthening it at home. It was a tremendous work of reorganization —administrative, economic, and social.

In order to ensure the defense of the frontiers, Leo III and his son began by coördinating the government of the *themes*, cutting up the huge administrative districts of the seventh century into a number of circumscriptions of smaller size and easier to defend; they derived therefrom the political advantage of diminishing the power which the possession of too vast territories gave to the *strategoi*, and of lessening the danger from the revolts which resulted from it. While the *Military Code* restored discipline in the army, a careful and often severe financial administration increased the resources of the treasury. The *Rural Code* aimed to restrain the disquieting development of the great domains, to arrest the disappearance of the small free estates, and to ensure to the peasants better living conditions. The *Nautical Code* encouraged the development of the merchant marine. But, above all, the great legislative reform which was marked by the publication of the civil code called the *Ecloga* (739) improved the administration of justice, and introduced into the law, together with greater clearness, a wholly new and more Christian spirit of humanity and equality. After a half-century of rule, the first two Isaurians had made the Empire rich and prosperous, despite the plague which ravaged it in 747, and despite the agitation caused by the iconoclastic controversy.

II. THE ICONOCLASTIC CONTROVERSY (726–780)

In order to complete their reconstructive work, Leo III and Constantine V attempted a great religious reform. They proscribed the holy images, persecuted the monks who constituted themselves their protectors, and from the serious conflict which they started, called the *Iconoclastic Controversy*, they have come to be known in history under the name of *Iconoclasts*.

The religious policy of the Isaurian emperors has often been misinterpreted, and its purpose and scope have been but imperfectly understood. The reasons that influenced them were at once religious and political. Many pious souls, at the beginning of the eighth century, were shocked by the excesses of superstition, particularly by the importance attributed to the worship of images, by the miracles which were expected of them, and by the manner in which they were involved in all human actions and concerns; and many good people were justly disturbed by the discredit which these practices brought upon religion. In Asia, especially, the hostile feeling against the images was strong; and Leo III, who was of Asiatic origin, shared in this feeling. Neither he nor his son was, as has sometimes been thought, a free-thinker, or rationalist, or precursor of the Reformation or the Revolution: they were men of their own time—pious, believers, even theologians, sincerely desirous of reforming religion and of purifying it of what seemed to them to be idolatry.

But they were statesmen, also, intent upon increasing the grandeur and tranquillity of the Empire. Now the greater number of monasteries, the constant growth of monastic wealth, were the source of grave dangers to the State. The immunity enjoyed by the possessions of the Church diminished the resources of the treasury. The multitude of men who entered the cloisters took laborers from the farms, soldiers from the army, and officials from the public service. But, above all, the influence that the monks exercised over men's minds, and the power that resulted therefrom, made them an element of dangerous unrest.

It was this state of affairs which the Isaurian emperors attempted to counteract: by proscribing the images, they aimed at the monks, who found in the images and in their cult the most powerful sanction for their acts. It is quite true, that, by the strife which they thus inaugurated, the Isaurian emperors started a long era of commotions; it is quite true that this struggle had very grave political consequences. We must not forget, however, if we would judge the iconoclastic sovereigns fairly, that in their undertaking they found numerous supporters among the higher clergy, who were jealous of the influence of the monks; in the army, which was composed mainly of Asiatics; and not only in official circles, but in a portion of the populace itself; and that the work which they undertook was not without cause or without great importance.

In 726 Leo III promulgated the first edict against the images, by which, it would seem, he ordered, not that they should be destroyed, but that they should be hung higher up, so as to remove them from the adoration of the multitude. This act aroused extreme excitement; there were acts of violence in Constantinople; a revolt—which was, however, quickly suppressed—in Greece (727); a general uprising in Italy (727); and while Pope Gregory II confined himself to protesting vigorously against the Iconoclastic heresy, his successor, Gregory III, soon inaugurated a bolder policy, and, not content with anathematizing the adversaries of the images (731), he sought temporarily the aid of the Lombards against the Emperor. In Syria, John of Damascus thundered with like zeal against Leo III. Nevertheless, the edict seems to have been executed with great moderation; there was no systematic persecution of the defenders of the images; and although the Patriarch Germanus was deposed, and replaced by a partisan of reform (729); although measures were taken against the ecclesiastical schools, the insurrection in Greece, on the other hand, was repressed without violence.

But the struggle was inevitably destined to become embittered. Questions of principle soon entered into a conflict wherein, in reality, the Emperor's authority in matters of religion, and the desire of the Church to free itself from the guardianship of the State, were brought face to face. Furthermore, Constantine V, who was more of a theologian than his father, carried into the conflict his personal opinions, which were no longer hostile to the images alone, but to the adoration of the Virgin and the intercession of the saints; and, as he was also more vehement in his faith, he conducted the strife with a more fanatical ardor, and with a more systematic and rigorous bitterness.

When, after ten glorious and prosperous years, he had made his throne secure, which had tottered momentarily before the revolt of Artavasdus (740–742), he convoked a council at Hieria (753), which solemnly condemned the images. Thenceforth, the prince was in a position to attack his adversaries, not only as rebels against the emperor, but as in revolt against God himself. Nevertheless, he flattered himself at first that he might be able to convince his adversaries by argument; so that the persecution did not really begin until 765. The images were destroyed, convents closed or secularized or transformed into barracks and inns; the property of the monasteries was confiscated; the monks were arrested, imprisoned, maltreated, and exiled; a few, like Saint Stephen the Younger, were condemned to death; others, in derision, were exhibited in grotesque processions to the people assembled in the Hippodrome. Several high dignitaries of the Empire were executed or banished. The Patriarch Constantine, being first banished, suffered capital punishment (767).

For five years the persecution raged throughout the Empire; not so terrible perhaps as the adversaries of the Emperor have represented,—death sentences seem, on the whole, to have been rare,—but, nevertheless, extremely violent. It seemed, says a contemporary, "that the purpose of the government was to extirpate utterly the monastic order." The monks resisted stubbornly; they suffered bravely "for justice and for truth." But many yielded, and many fled, especially to Italy, so that, as a contemporary,—with some exaggeration, no doubt,—observes, "Byzantium seemed to be left without any monastic order."

It is certain that the contest was the occasion of

acts of indescribable violence and savagery and of nameless cruelties, and that it caused a tremendous excitement in the Empire. It had, moreover, very momentous consequences. Already Leo III, by attempting to put down the opposition of the Papacy by force, by detaching Calabria, Sicily, Crete, and western Illyricum (732) from obedience to Rome, and placing them under the rule of the Patriarch of Constantinople, had aggravated the discontent of the popes and the disaffection of Italy. When, in 751, the Exarchate of Ravenna succumbed under the blows of the Lombards, Pope Stephen II did not hesitate to detach himself from the Empire,—heretical as it was, and powerless to defend the peninsula,—and to seek with the Franks a protection less onerous and more effective; and he accepted from the victorious Pepin territories formerly belonging to Byzantium, which formed, thenceforth, the temporal domain of the Papacy (754). This meant a rupture between Rome and the Empire.

Constantine V spared no pains to punish one in whom he could see only a treacherous and disloyal subject, illegitimately usurping that which belonged to his master. His efforts were fruitless. In 774, Charlemagne, intervening once more in the affairs of the peninsula, solemnly confirmed the donation of Pepin. Byzantium retained nothing in Italy except Venice and a few towns in the southern part of the peninsula. And although, because of this, the diminished Empire was thrown back still a little more toward the East, in this rupture were germinating the seeds of threatening complications and grave perils in the future.

BYZANTINE EMPIRE

THE religious policy of the first Isaurians had scattered abroad many germs of dissension, discontent, and ferment. These became manifest after the death of Constantine V.

During his short tenure of power, Leo IV (775–780) carried on the tradition of the preceding reign. But immediately after his death, his widow, Irene, regent for the young Constantine VI, deemed it more useful for her ambition to rely upon the orthodox, and to restore the worship of the images. In order to devote herself wholly to her great design, she neglected the war against the Mussulmans, who came back in 782 as far as Chrysopolis, opposite Constantinople; and she concluded a most humiliating peace with the Caliph, in 783. On the other hand, she made overtures to the Papacy, and established cordial relations with the Frankish kingdom; above all, at home she devoted herself to removing from the government the adversaries of the images, and banished her brothers-in-law, the sons of Constantine V; and having thus cleared the path, with the assistance of the Patriarch Tarasius she caused the iconoclastic heresy to be solemnly condemned at the Œcumenical Council of Nicæa (787), and restored the worship of the images, amid the applause of the faction of bigots, who saw in this triumph assurance of the proximate complete independence of the Church with respect to the State.

Intoxicated by her victory, and encouraged by the popularity that her pious zeal won for her, Irene did not hesitate to enter into a contest with her son, who had reached his majority, and to dispute his claim to the throne. The first time, in face of the discontent of the army, which remained faithful to the memory of Constantine V and, too, was exasperated by the defeats which the Arabs, Bulgars, and Lombards inflicted upon the imperial troops, she had no choice but to go into retirement (790). But with persistent craft she paved the way for her return to power: in 797 she overthrew her son, and did not shrink from having his eyes put out. From that time she reigned as a veritable emperor (797–802), the first woman who had as yet ruled the Empire in her own name.

But although, thanks to her, the Church, rehabilitated by the struggle, regained its place in Byzantine society; although the monastic and bigoted party, led by men like Theodore of Studion, became more powerful and aggressive than ever, yet the too exclusive attention which Irene paid to the religious question entailed consequences disastrous for the Empire. Despite the temporary successes gained by Constantine VI against the Arabs and Bulgarians (791–795), the Caliphate of Bagdad, under the government of Harun-al-Raschid, triumphantly renewed the offensive in the East, and compelled the Byzantines to pay him tribute (798). In the West, confronted by Charlemagne, the Greek government showed the same weakness; and the great event of the year 800, which restored the Roman Empire in the West for the behoof of the Frankish King, was a poignant humiliation for the Byzantine Court.

Shorn of part of its domain abroad, the Empire was

enfeebled at home by the too great partiality which the government showed the Church, by the deep-seated schisms which the Iconoclastic Controversy had left behind, and, lastly, by the bad example which Irene had set, in reopening the era of dynastic revolutions. True, the Iconoclastic epoch was marked by great intellectual and artistic progress. The Isaurian emperors were not puritanical: while proscribing the images, they loved ostentation and the worldly glamour of court life; and for the better decoration of their buildings, they encouraged a profane art, inspired by ancient tradition as well as by Arab models; and by this means, as well as through the prominence of the Asiatics in the eighth century, the Empire had become completely orientalized.

But, great as was the part which the Empire played as the champion of Christianity against Islam, as guardian of civilization against barbarism, it was, at the end of the eighth century, threatened on all sides by formidable perils, and it was very weak. The fall of Irene, who was overthrown by the *coup-d'état* of Nicephorus (802), opened the door to disaster and anarchy.

IV. THE SECOND PERIOD OF THE ICONOCLASTIC CONTROVERSY (802–824)

NICEPHORUS (802–811) was an intelligent prince, an able financier, desirous of repairing the impoverishment of the treasury, even if he were, to that end, compelled to seize Church property. He was moderate in his ideas, and repudiated the violence of the Iconoclasts; but none the less he planned to maintain their reforms; and, above all, he deemed inadmissible the aspirations of the Byzantine Church, which, intoxicated by its victory, aimed frankly at shaking off the authority of the State, and regaining its liberty. This is the characteristic aspect of the second phase of the Iconoclastic Controversy; there took place then in Byzantium something very like the Investiture Controversy in the West.

The monks of the monastery of St. John of Studion, under the leadership of their abbot, Theodore, were the most embittered and the most obstinate in supporting the claims of the Church. With equal bitterness they combatted the wise opportunism of the Patriarch Nicephorus (806–815), who endeavored to efface the memories of the Iconoclastic struggle, the financial policy of the Emperor, and his authority in respect of religion. The government was obliged to take severe measures against them (809), to disperse and banish them. The monks did not hesitate to appeal to the Pope, being ready to acknowledge the primacy of the Roman Church, provided that they could, at that price, ensure the independence of the Eastern Church with respect to the State. This attitude inevitably provoked an Iconoclastic reaction. This was the work of Leo V, the Armenian (813–820), and of the two emperors of the Phrygian dynasty, Michael II (820–829) and Theophilus (829–842). Again, for thirty years, the Empire was in the throes of a most violent convulsion.

In 815 a council assembled at Saint Sophia again proscribed the images and revived in full force the Iconoclastic decrees of 753. Consequently, the destruction of the images recommenced; above all, by means of condemnation, persecution, and exile, they pitilessly suppressed the demonstrations and opposition of the monks. Theodore of Studion died in exile (826); and the persecution was still more severe under the rule of the Emperor Theophilus, an ardent Iconoclast and bigoted theologian. A rigorous edict against the partisans of the images was promulgated in 832, and the Patriarch John, called Lekanomantis, undertook to execute it. Convents were closed, monks were persecuted and imprisoned, and terror reigned anew.

But, after one hundred and twenty years of fighting, men became weary of this exhausting and futile strife. After the death of Theophilus, the regent Theodora, his widow, on the advice of her brother Bardas, decided to bring about peace by restoring the worship of the images. This was the work of the Council of 843, over which the new Patriarch Methodius presided, and whose decisions were proclaimed in a solemn ceremony, which, to this day, the Greek Church commemorates on the nineteenth of February, in the annual festival of orthodoxy (Κυριακὴ τῆς ὀρθοδοξίας).

But, although the images were restored, although the Church was victorious in this respect, the work of the Iconoclastic emperors remained intact as to the essential point. They had aimed to keep the Church independence on the State, to increase the imperial power over it; the Studites had fought bitterly against these pretensions; they had obstinately denied to the emperor the right to decide concerning the dogmas of the faith, and had unyieldingly maintained the Church's independence of lay authority. On this point the Studites were vanquished. The Iconoclastic controversy had the undeniable result of making the Church more submissive than ever to the authority of the emperor.

V. THE FOREIGN POLICY OF THE EMPIRE AND THE RECONSTRUCTION OF THE MONARCHY (802–867)

WHILE the Empire was thus absorbed in these religious struggles, grave events disturbed its internal tranquillity, and endangered its security from without.

The crime of Irene against her son, by removing the Isaurian dynasty from the throne, had reopened the era of revolutions. The *coup d'état* which placed Nicephorus on the throne (802) was followed by the pronunciamento that elevated Leo V (813) and the conspiracy which, after assassinating Leo V, put in his place Michael II (820). In addition to the plots that succeeded, there was a long series of attempts that failed, of which the most formidable was the rebellion of Thomas (822–824), who, seeking support among the lower classes, imparted to his uprising an almost socialistic aspect. For twenty years the country was a prey to anarchy.

Affairs were in scarcely better case externally. The treaty of 812, which recognized Charlemagne as Emperor, confirmed the loss of Italy, where Byzantium retained only Venice and a few districts in the southern part of the peninsula. The war with the Arabs, which broke out again in 804, resulted in two grave disasters, the occupation of Crete by Mussulman corsairs from Spain (826),—who, from that base, ravaged, almost with impunity, the eastern Mediterranean,—and the conquest of Sicily (827) by the Arabs of Africa, who, in 831, captured Palermo. But the Bulgarian peril was most to be dreaded, since the redoubtable Khan Kroumi had extended his empire from the Balkans to the Carpathians. Nicephorus endeavored to hold him in check by invading Bulgaria; on his return thence, he perished in a sanguinary defeat (811), and the Bulgarians, again victorious at Adrianople, made their way to the very walls of Constantinople (813). The victory of Leo V at Mesembria (817) saved the Empire. But, if we reflect that to all these diverse perils were added the insurrections of half-conquered peoples, like the Slavs of the Peloponnesus (807), we can understand that, after twenty years of anarchy, the work of the great Isaurian emperors seemed to be utterly destroyed.

Nevertheless, the Empire survived this crisis. The reign of Theophilus (819–842) repaired in part the disasters suffered in the East, thanks to the increasing weakness of the Caliphate of Bagdad; and even though, in truth, after the defeat at Dazimon (the present Tokat), and the capture of Amorion (838), it was necessary to sue for peace to the Arabs, still, through the energy of her internal government, her wise financial administration, and the skill of her diplomacy, Byzantium recovered her prestige and her prosperity. In the magnificence of its buildings, in the splendor of the Sacred Palace, in the preëminence of its civilization, Constantinople, toward the middle of the ninth century, rivaled the capital of the caliphs. And when, at last, the interminable Iconoclastic Controversy was brought to an end, she appeared even more brilliant and powerful. On her emergence from the long period of convulsions, literature and art seemed to take on fresh vigor; and the University of Constantinople, reëstablished in the palace of Magnaura by Cæsar Bardas (about 850), became once more, under the direction of Leo of Thessalonica, the centre of a notable intellectual culture.

At the same time, the Church, coming forth rejuvenated from the struggle, placed its renewed activity at the service of the State. It restored religious unity, by combatting heresy, especially that of the Paulicians, which the government of Theodora persecuted severely in Asia Minor; and by achieving the conversion of the Slavs of the Peloponnesus (849); above all, by the work of its missions, it extended wonderfully the influence of Byzantium throughout the East. At the call of the Prince of Great Moravia, Cyril and Methodius, "the apostles of the Slavs," carried Christianity to the savage tribes that dwelt in Hungary and Bohemia (863). They did even more: for the benefit of the new converts they translated the Holy Scriptures into Slavic; for transcribing their work, they invented the Glagolitic alphabet, and thus gave to the Slavs both their alphabet and their literary language; they preached in Slavic, they celebrated the offices in the Slavic tongue and with a Slavic liturgy; they strove to organize a Slavic clergy; and by these wise and tactful methods, they won over the Slavic peoples to the orthodox faith. For twenty years (863–885) the two brothers of Thessalonica pursued their work of evangelization in Moravia. And although it finally succumbed before German hostility and the Magyar invasion, elsewhere these same methods procured for Byzantium more durable triumphs. Christianity made its way into the Jewish state of the Khazars, on the banks of the Don. Most important of all, in 864, Boris, Tsar of Bulgaria, became a convert to the orthodox faith; and, although in the years following the neophyte wavered for a moment between Byzantium and Rome; although he had entered into relations with Pope Nicholas I, to request from him the introduction of ritual into his realm (866), none the less Greek influence became thereafter deeply rooted in Bulgaria.

These were great achievements. Undoubtedly the follies of Michael III (842–867), especially after the young prince escaped from the tutelage of his mother Theodora (856) and his uncle Bardas, endangered temporarily the results thus obtained. The piracies of the Arabs of Crete swept eastern waters bare; in Asia Minor, during twenty years (844–863), victories alternated with reverses. In the West, the Mussulmans completed the conquest of Sicily between 843 and 859. Finally, the Russians appeared before Constantinople in 860, for the first time; and, in the popular belief, it required nothing less than a miracle of the Virgin to save the capital.

Another event of more serious significance marked the reign of Michael III. In place of Ignatius, deposed by Cæsar Bardas, Photius had become Patriarch of Constantinople (858). The Pope, Nicholas I, at the entreaty of the deposed prelate, took cognizance of the affair and charged his legates to open an investigation. The ambition of Photius was at no loss to exploit in marvelous measure the discontent with which for centuries the Orient had regarded the pretensions of the pope, and the hostility that it cherished against the West: as against the claims of the Roman primacy, he shrewdly succeeded in making his personal cause a veritable national cause. To the excommunication that Nicholas I hurled against him in 863, he responded by breaking with Rome. The Council of Constantinople (867) anathematized the Pope, denounced his illegal interference in the affairs of the Eastern Church, and consummated the schism. It was a striking proof of the existence of a national Byzantine sentiment, which showed itself about the same time, in no less unequivocal fashion, in the feeling caused by the encroaching policy of Rome in Bulgaria (866).

Thus, toward the middle of the ninth century, there really existed a Byzantine nationality, which had slowly taken shape in the midst of passing events; the Empire, at the end of the Iconoclastic Controversy had recovered religious unity, political power, and intellectual eminence; above all, it had become a strictly Oriental Empire. The moment was at hand when this Empire was to reach the apex of its greatness. When Basil the Macedonian,[1] the favorite of Michael III, and associated with him on the throne, had rid himself of his rival Bardas (866), he next assassinated his benefactor (867), and thus raised a new dynasty to power. By this *coup d'état* he gave one hundred and fifty years of splendor, prosperity, and renown to the Byzantine Empire.

[1] This is his usual designation; but we must note that the family of Basil was of Armenian origin, and had been very recently transplanted in Macedonia.

CHAPTER V

The Apogee of the Empire under the Macedonian Dynasty, 867-1081

I. THE SOVEREIGNS OF THE MACEDONIAN LINE AND THE CONSOLIDATION OF THE DYNASTY

FROM 867 to 1025 the Byzantine Empire knew nearly one hundred and sixty years of incomparable splendor. For a century and a half, it had the good fortune to have at its head a succession of sovereigns nearly all of whom were remarkable men. Basil I, the founder of the dynasty (867–886), Romanus (I) Lecapenus (919–944), Nicephorus (II) Phocas (963–969), John (I) Tzimisces (969–979),—illustrious usurpers, who ruled under the name of legitimate princes,—and, lastly, Basil II, who reigned for a whole half century (976–1025), were not such men as historians are only too ready to represent the Byzantine emperors to have been. These were vigorous men, of stern mould, often unscrupulous and pitiless, strong-willed and imperious, more intent upon inspiring fear than upon inspiring love; but they were statesmen, passionately preoccupied with the grandeur of the Empire; illustrious warriors, whose lives were passed in camps, among soldiers, in whom they recognized and loved the source of imperial power. They were skilful administrators, of persistent and inflexible energy, who hesitated at nothing when the public welfare was in question. They had no liking for useless expenditure, they were intent solely upon increasing the national wealth; the glittering luxury of the palace, the empty pomp of processions and ceremonials interested them only in so far as these things furthered their policies, and upheld the prestige of the emperor and the empire. Jealous of their authority, they had, generally speaking, no favorites; if we except such a powerful personality as the Grand Chamberlain Basil, illegitimate son of Romanus Lecapenus, who was through five reigns and for more than forty years (944–988) the soul of the government, their advisers were in most cases obscure men, whom they employed, and whose masters they always were. Enamoured of renown, and with their hearts filled with the highest ambitions, they aimed to make the Byzantine Empire the predominant power in the Oriental world, champion at once of Hellenism and of the orthodox faith; and, by their glorious exploits of arms, by the supple shrewdness of their diplomacy, and by the vigor of their government, they realized their dream, and made of this period an epoch of veritable rebirth, one of the most resplendent moments in the long history of Byzantium.

At the moment when Basil I ascended the throne, the situation of the monarchy was still peculiarly difficult. It seemed that the whole state must be made over. The uncultivated peasant, whose crime had elevated him to the supreme power, had all the qualities necessary to accomplish this stupendous task: he was intelligent; equally desirous of reëstablishing good order in the interior of the monarchy and of restoring its prestige abroad; an excellent administrator, a good soldier, ambitious, above all, to establish the imperial authority on a solid foundation. During his reign of twenty years he was able to place the affairs of the empire on a favorable footing, and at the same time, through the prestige of services rendered, to ensure the fortune of his family.

His son, Leo VI (886–912), whose reign occupies an important place in the administrative history of the Empire, different as he was from his father by reason of his rough-and-ready character, his pedantic whims, and his weakness in dealing with his favorites, pursued with the same tenacity the consolidation of the dynasty. In order to ensure an heir to the throne, he did not shrink from scandalizing his contemporaries by his four marriages, or from entering into a conflict with the Church and its head, the Patriarch Nicholas. But, at this price, there came into being, for the first time in Byzantium, for the benefit of a reigning family, the idea of legitimation. It was the preëminent work of the first two Macedonian emperors, "to furnish," so writes a contemporary, "robust roots to the imperial authority, in order that the superb branches of the dynasty may spring therefrom." Thereafter it was more difficult to uproot the tree so firmly embedded in the soil; thereafter there was an imperial family, whose members received the name of *Porphyrogeniti;* and there grew up a popular attachment, a loyal devotion to that family. In that monarchy, previously kept in a turmoil by so many revolutions, this was a fortunate novelty, pregnant with consequences.

To be sure, even during this period there was no lack of revolutions. The commotions that marked the disturbed minority of Constantine VII, the son of Leo VI (912–959), enabled Romanus Lecapenus to usurp power for a quarter of a century (919–944). A little later, when Romanus II, son of Constantine VII, died after reigning four years (959–963), the weakness of the government during the minority of his sons, Basil II and Constantine VIII, led to the uprising which bore Nicephorus Phocas into power (963–969), and to the tragic *coup d'état* which, by the assassination of Nicephorus, made John Tzimisces Emperor (969–976).

But no one of these usurpers dared to exclude from the throne the legitimate descendants of Basil I. Romanus Lecapenus officially shared the power with Constantine VII, although in reality he relegated him to the obscure leisure of his studious activity as a scholar. Nicephorus Phocas and John Tzimisces allowed the children of Romanus II to reign nominally, and endeavored, by espousing princesses of the imperial family, to give an air of legitimacy to their usurpation. And after them the power devolved again naturally upon the representative, now past his minority, of the Macedonian family—the great Emperor, Basil II. The dynasty was so firmly established that in this Oriental monarchy even women could reign—the nieces of Basil II, Zoë (1028–1050), who shared the throne with her three successve husbands, and Theodora (1054–1056); and these princesses were popular,—witness the revolution of 1042, when Michael V was deposed for attempting to dethrone Zoë, and the disaffection that Constantine Monomachus encountered when he was suspected of wishing to set aside the two empresses. Nothing of the kind had ever before been known in Byzantium, and public opinion declared openly that "he who finally reigns in Constantinople is always victorious"—which made usurpation not only a crime, but, even worse, a blunder.

As it happened, however, that the usurpers also were eminent men and notable generals, the Empire was able to endure without mishap the political incapacity of a Constantine VII, the dissipation of Romanus II, and the long minority of his sons, and to maintain, during a century and a half, in the conduct of its affairs, a unity of aims and a firm guidance of which Byzantium had had no experience for many years.

Furthermore, by favor of the assistance of collaborators of high merit,—generals like the Kurkuas, the Phocases, and the Scleruses, and ministers like the Grand Chamberlain Basil,—the emperors of the Macedonian dynasty were able to bestow upon the monarchy a vast increase of territory and an incomparable splendor. The offensive resumed on all frontiers, and crowned with brilliant successes; diplomacy complementing the military operations and gathering around the monarchy an escort of vassals; the Byzantine influence spreading throughout the whole eastern world, and far into the west; a strong government, distinguished by great legislative achievements; a centralized administration, skilful and judicious, which, by the common stamp of Hellenism, and by the common profession of the orthodox faith, was able to ensure to the Empire that unity which the diversity of races seemed to deny it—these things were what Byzantium owed to the hundred and fifty years during which the Macedonian emperors held sway.

And even if they were not able, notwithstanding their efforts, to avert the formidable perils that menaced this prosperity; to solve the agrarian and social problem, which was distressingly acute; to checkmate the feudal aristocracy, always quick to revolt; to prevent the ambitious heads of the Eastern Church from inciting to schism, and, by separating Byzantium from Rome forever, impairing the solidity of the Empire; even if the dying Macedonian dynasty left an Empire powerless to oppose the Normans and the Turks, and opened the door to a long period of anarchy (1057–1081)—nevertheless, for a century and a half, the dynasty founded by Basil I conferred extraordinary glory upon Byzantium. In the tenth and eleventh centuries, Constantinople was the most brilliant centre of European civilization, and, as someone has said, "the Paris of the Middle Ages."

II. THE FOREIGN POLICY OF THE MACEDONIAN EMPERORS (867–1025)

The War Against the Arabs.—Since the Arabs had conquered Crete, in 826, they had become the scourge of the waters about Byzantium. Candia, the capital of the island, was the lair of Mussulman pirates, and from thence, as well as from Tarsus or from Tripoli in Syria, Arab corsairs ravaged the whole Ægean Sea.

Despite the efforts of Basil I to reorganize the army and the fleet, the enemy squadrons dominated the Archipelago. In 904, Thessalonica was taken by Leo of Tripoli, and almost its whole population was led away into captivity. Despite a few successes of the Byzantine navy in 907, and later in 924, in the waters about Lemnos, the expeditions against Crete resulted only in disaster (911 and 949). It was found necessary to send against the island "accursed of God" the best general of the Empire, Nicephorus Phocas (960). He succeeded in landing in Crete, and after a siege of several months, he carried Candia by assault (March, 961). The conquered island was converted to Christianity. The mastery of the eastern waters reverted to the Byzantines.

At the same time, a happy turn of affairs permitted the resumption of the offensive in Asia Minor. Basil I had already extended the boundaries of the Empire to the upper Euphrates, had recaptured Samosata (873), and had made victorious campaigns in Cappadocia and Cilicia (878–879). The confusion in the Mussulman world in the tenth century facilitated still more the victories of the Byzantines, especially when, after 927, the Empire was delivered from the Bulgarian peril. The war was actively pressed under illustrious generals—John Kurkuas, who commanded in Asia Minor for twenty-two years (920–942), and deserved to be called "another Trajan, another Belisarius;" then under Bardas Phocas and his sons, Nicephorus, Leo, and Constantine. In 928, Theodosiopolis, the present Erzerum, was taken; in 934, Melitene; in 944, Edessa, whence they bore away in triumph the miraculous image of Christ which was preserved there; in 949, Germanikia; in 957, Amida; in 958, Samosata. The Byzantine frontier was advanced from the Halys to the Euphrates and Tigris, and a series of newly organized provinces (the *themes* of Sebaste, Mesopotamia, Seleucia, and Lycandos) attested the importance of the Byzantine conquests. Armenia and Iberia shook off the yoke of Islam, and entered the Byzantine sphere of influence. Throughout the tenth century the Armenians were destined to play an important part in the affairs of the monarchy, and to supply it with soldiers, generals, administrators, diplomats, and even emperors: Romanus Lecapenus and John Tzimisces were both of Armenian origin.

A genuine crusading movement impelled the Byzantines against the infidels. In Cilicia and in northern Syria Nicephorus Phocas crushed the power of the Hamdanid emirs of Aleppo. He captured Anazarbus, Adana, Mopsuestia (964), Tarsus (965), Laodicea, Hieropolis, Emesa, Aleppo, and, finally, Antioch (968). His successor, John Tzimisces, conquered Edessa and Nisibis in Mesopotamia (974), Damascus and Beirut in Syria (976), and in Palestine approached the gates of Jerusalem. "And the people," says a chronicler, "feared the wrath of Tzimisces, and the sword of the Christians mowed down the infidels as with a scythe."

Basil II completed this reconquest of the Orient. In 995 he took Aleppo, Homs, and Schaizar. Magnificent triumphs celebrated the downfall of the Mussulman power; the Empire extended its boundaries in the east, and was powerfully defended against every fresh aggression by a chain of strong fortresses. The annexation, perhaps not altogether wise, of the Armenian principalities by Basil II (1020), and the submission of Iberia completed these glorious conquests. Since the time of Justinian, the authority of the Empire had never stretched so far toward the East.

The War Against the Bulgarians.—Even more than the Arab war, the Bulgarian war is of capital importance in the external history of Byzantium in the tenth century.

At the beginning of that century the Bulgarian menace was more formidable than ever. Territorially, the Bulgarian state extended from the regions north of the Danube to the Balkan Peninsula, and to the west it reached as far as the peaks of the Pindus. Morally, by the fusion, now complete, of the Bulgarian and Slav elements, Bulgaria formed a homogeneous state, where the monarchical power was strongly developed; where conversion to Christianity assured unity of faith; where, through contact with Byzantium, the country had risen to quite a high degree of civilization. And all this tempted the Bulgarian sovereigns to dispute with the Byzantine emperors the hegemony of the Balkans.

To realize these ambitious dreams, it was enough that one man should come to the front: this man was the son of Boris, the Tsar Symeon (893–927). Educated at Byzantium, where he had been held as a hostage, and deeply enamoured of the magnificence and the civilization of the Byzantines, he dreamed of conquering Constantinople, and of placing on his own head the crown of Constantine's successors. For more than a century a genuine race-war was waged between Greeks and Bulgarians.

The war began in 889, and, strange to say, the causes were economic in their nature. When Leo VI ordered the warehouses of the Bulgarian merchants in Constantinople to be removed to Thessalonica, Symeon declared war. An invasion of the Hungarians, subsidized by the Byzantines, finally forced the Bulgarian King to retreat (893). But after the death of Leo VI, the disturbances that marked the minority of Constantine VII gave him an opportunity to return. In 913 he appeared before Constantinople; in 914 he took Adrianople; in 917 he crushed the imperial armies in the battle of Anchialus.

Intoxicated by success, Symeon proclaimed himself "Tsar of the Bulgarians and Emperor of the Romans." He installed an independent Bulgarian patriarchate in his capital of Preslav; it only remained for him to take Constantinople. He attempted it in 924. But to take the Byzantine capital, it was necessary to attack it both by land and by sea, and Symeon had no navy. It appears, also, that in the interview that he had with Romanus Lecapenus, like Attila before St. Leo, he submitted to the influence of all the prestige and civilization of that ancient imperial majesty. He retreated, he abandoned the golden dream he had cherished. And although, in his own kingdom, especially in Preslav the Great, his capital, Symeon had fostered an intellectual and artistic culture which has earned for him the name of the Charlemagne of Bulgaria, the check at Constantinople marked the downfall of Bulgarian ambition. When Symeon died (927), the decadence had already begun. It continued at increased speed in the long reign of his son Peter (927–968). During those forty years Bulgaria became more and more a satellite of the Empire; and while Byzantium grew stronger, her ancient rival grew weaker day by day. In face of the waning royal power, feudalism again raised its head; religious unity was endangered by the heresy of the Bogomiles; the Bulgarian nationality was disintegrating. The Byzantines' hour of revenge was at hand.

It struck in 967. Nicephorus Phocas refused the tribute which the Empire had always paid to the Bulgarians, and, with the aid of the Russians under Sviatoslaff, the Grand Prince of Kiev, he attacked Bulgaria. But Sviatoslaff found the conquered land greatly to his taste; he settled there, and refused to leave (968). The death of the Tsar Peter and the assassination of Nicephorus (969) increased the difficulties of the situation. When John Tzimisces ascended the throne, the Russian invasion was threatening the Empire itself: Sviatoslaff crossed the Balkans, sacked Philippopolis (970), and spread panic as far as the capital. Luckily, the Russians were beaten at Arcadiopolis, the present Lulé-Bourgas (970), and the Emperor had time to organize a great expedition against them (971). While the Byzantine fleet sailed up the Danube, Tzimisces crossed the Balkans, took Preslav, besieged Sviatoslaff in Dorostol (Silistria), and obliged him to submit and to evacuate the country. Bulgaria was annexed to the Empire, and the autonomous patriarchate was suppressed; victorious Hellenism carried the boundaries of the Empire to the banks of the Danube.

Nevertheless, in the Bulgaria of the Pindus, about Prespa and Ochrida, the national element, under the leadership of Count Sischman and his sons, resisted obstinately. Under cover of the commotions that disturbed the early days of the reign of Basil II, one of Sischman's sons, the Tsar Samuel (from between 977 and 979 to 1014) reconstituted Bulgaria. In ten years, from 977 to 986, he liberated Danubian Bulgaria, conquered Macedonia and Thessaly, even forced his way into the Peloponnesus. It required thirty years of war (986–1018) for the Greeks to overthrow this redoubtable empire, which extended from the Danube to the Adriatic. This was substantially the work of the Emperor Basil II, whose unrelenting energy and cruel victories won for him the terrible nickname of *Bulgaroctonos* — the slayer of Bulgarians.

In 986 Basil II took the offensive and penetrated into Bulgaria; but he was badly beaten at the pass of the Trajan Gate in the Balkans. Ten years passed before the Emperor was able to resume the struggle, and during those ten years Samuel continued to add to the extent of his kingdom, from the Danube to the Adriatic and to the Ægean Sea. But in 996 the Tsar was defeated on the banks of the Sperchius, and Greece was lost to him; he failed before Thessalonica, and a part of Danubian Bulgaria fell into the hands of the imperial troops (1000). But Western Bulgaria was impregnable. In 1001, Basil II undertook to subdue it. One after another, he conquered the adjacent territories—Berrhœa, Servia, Vodena. Surrounded in the mountains, Samuel extricated himself and sacked Adrianople (1003). But the Emperor pursued him unrelentingly, and drew the net closer, taking Skopi, conquering lower and middle Macedonia (1007), and carrying on the war with savage brutality. Samuel avoided pitched battles; finally, however, his troops were crushed at the pass of Kimbalongou, on the road from Seres to Melnik (July 29, 1014). The Tsar did not survive this defeat: he died a few days later (September 15, 1014). This was the end of Bulgaria.

To be sure, the successors of the great Bulgarian Tsar, while quarrelling over his throne, continued the war for a further period of four years. But in 1018 the country was wholly pacified and the Emperor, in a triumphal tour, set about reconstructing it. He did this with wisdom and tact, respecting the customs and governmental methods of the vanquished, trying to win over the great feudal aristocracy, and preserving the ancient religious organization, which had at its head the *autocephalous* Archbishop of Ochrida.

Thus, after many years, Byzantium again became mistress of the whole Balkan Peninsula; and in the journey that he made through Greece, as far as Athens, as well as in the triumph which he celebrated with great pomp at Constantinople (1019), Basil II could fairly boast of having restored the Empire to a height of power it had not known for centuries.

The Recovery of Southern Italy and the Byzantine Policy in the West.—While the princes of the Macedonian line were gloriously pushing forward the frontiers of the Empire in the East, in the West they resumed the ambitious traditions of Byzantine statecraft. The Byzantines had never renounced their claim of dominion over Italy. Memories of Rome, the ancient capital of the Roman sphere, and of Ravenna, the ancient capital of the exarchate, haunted their dreams incessantly. The weakness of the last Carolingian emperors, the anarchy in southern Italy, divided between the Lombard princes, and the increasing menace of the Mussulman offensive, gave Basil II the desired excuse for intervention in the peninsula and for attempting to realize his ambitions.

The Emperor had taken upon himself the task of reviving the prestige of Byzantium throughout the Mediterranean, of driving the Mussulman corsairs from the Adriatic and from the Tyrrhenian Sea, and of fighting the Saracens of Africa and Sicily. From the time of his accession, then, he pursued a vigorous policy in the West. It is true that he did not succeed in recovering Sicily, where Syracuse fell into the hands of the infidels, in 878. But he restored order in the Adriatic, renewed the Byzantine alliance with Venice, and brought the Croats back into vassalage to Greece. Above all, he reoccupied Bari (876) and Tarentum (860), reconquered Calabria (885), and imposed a Byzantine protectorate upon the Lombard princes. Two new *themes*, those of Longobardia and Calabria, were formed in southern Italy. It was a notable compensation for the loss of Sicily.

The weakness of Leo VI endangered momentarily

these fortunate results. Having achieved the conquest of Sicily by the capture of Taormina (902), the Arabs were able to invade Calabria, and even to establish themselves in Campania. The victory of Garigliano (915) assured anew Byzantine supremacy in Italy, and, during a whole century, despite the persistence of Saracen invasions and the rivalry of the German emperors, the Greeks maintained their authority throughout the southern half of Italy. There, too, the glorious reign of Basil II brought to consummation the ambitions of the Macedonian dynasty.

The victory of Cannes (1018), won by the imperial troops over the rebellious tribes of Apulia, restored Byzantine prestige, from Reggio and Bari up to the gates of the Papal States. And under the imperial government, skilful in spreading the influence of Hellenism, southern Italy, thanks above all to its Greek clergy and Greek convents, became a veritable *Græcia Magna*—a remarkable proof of the power of expansion, and of the force of the civilization that assimilates, which constituted the greatness of the Byzantine Empire in the tenth and eleventh centuries.

But the entry on the scene of the German Emperors, about the middle of the tenth century, hampered to some extent the Byzantine policy. When Otto went down into Italy, when he assumed the title of Emperor, Greek pride endured with impatience what seemed to it a usurpation. It was even worse when Otto extended his suzerainty over the Lombard princes, vassals of Byzantium; when he invaded Grecian territory and attacked Bari (968). Nicephorus Phocas retaliated vigorously. But his death modified the Byzantine policy: an agreement supervened, which was confirmed by the marriage of Otto II and Theophano (972). Nevertheless, the good understanding lasted only a short time; German ambitions could not be reconciled with the Byzantine demands. But the German emperors had little success: Otto II invaded Calabria, and was defeated at Stilo (987); Henry II resisted in vain the Apulian revolt, and failed in his attacks on Greek Italy (1022). At the death of Basil II, Byzantium was all-powerful in Italy, as well as in Asia and Bulgaria.

Diplomacy: the vassals of the Empire.—Thanks to its great military successes, the Greek Empire, in the tenth century, extended from the Danube to Syria, and from the shores of Italy to the plains of Armenia. But clever diplomacy was destined to extend its sphere of influence far beyond these limits. All about the Empire was grouped a succession of vassal states, which formed a first line of defense beyond the frontier, and, above all, spread proudly through the world the political influence and the civilization of Byzantium.

In Italy, Venice, wholly Greek in origin and in customs, was the most faithful and the most docile of the vassals of the Empire. The emperors had, therefore, entrusted to her the task of policing the Adriatic; and from the end of the tenth century (992) they had granted her those ample commercial privileges which paved the way for her future greatness. In southern Italy the republics of Naples, Gaeta, and Amalfi revolved in the orbit of Byzantium; lastly, the Lombard princes of Salerno, Capua, and Beneventum, although of less assured fidelity, accepted, generally the Greek protectorate. In the northwest of the Balkan Peninsula and along the whole shore of the Adriatic, the Slavic states of Croatia and Serbia, brought back by Basil I to Christianity and the authority of Byzantium, were useful allies of the Empire, particularly against the Bulgarians. In the East, on the shore of the Black Sea, Cherson, a vassal rather than a subject state, was a valuable post of observation and means of political and economic action against the barbarian tribes — Khazars, Petchenegs, and Russians — which inhabited the neighboring steppes. In the Caucasus, the princes of the Alani, the Abasges, and Albania, took pride in bearing the titles and receiving the subsidies of Byzantium. And, finally, the states of Armenia, wrested in the tenth century from Arab influence, furnished the Empire with generals and soldiers by the thousand. The Bagratid King of Armenia, too, as well as the princes of Vasparokan, Taron, and Iberia, were faithful adherents and retainers of the Empire, pending the time when their domains should be annexed, one after another, by Basil II.

Religious Policy: The Conversion of Russia.—But outside of these regions brought under the Greek protectorate, the civilizing influence of Byzantium extended still farther. As always, the missionaries seconded the work of the diplomats. Of this fact, the conversion of the Russians to Christianity offers a striking proof.

Since the middle of the ninth century Byzantium

had had relations with Russia. Several times after the aggressive enterprise of 860, adventurers from Kiev had threatened Constantinople with their attacks (907 and 941); on the other hand, the emperors freely recruited soldiers from among these fearless fighters, and Russian merchants traded in the Byzantine market. The visit of the Tsarina Olga to Byzantium (957), and her conversion to Christianity, made these relations even closer.

But the conversion of Vladimir, Great Prince of Kiev, at the end of the tenth century, was the most decisive event of all. In 988, in order to subdue the feudal uprisings, Basil II obtained from the Prince of Kiev a force of six thousand mercenaries; in exchange, Vladimir requested the hand of a Byzantine princess; and, the better to stimulate the wavering will of the imperial court, he seized Cherson. Basil II acceded to the demands of the barbarian prince, but persuaded him to receive baptism. Vladimir was baptized at Cherson (989), then imposed Christianity upon his people at Kiev. And Russia, thenceforth a Christian nation, formed herself on the model of Byzantine civilization; she borrowed from Byzantium, together with the orthodox faith, her art, her literature, and her manners. After Vladimir, his son Yaroslaff (1015–1054) continued and consummated the work, and made of Kiev, his capital, the rival of Constantinople, and one of the most beautiful cities in the Orient. Vladimir was the Clovis of Russia; Yaroslaff was her Charlemagne. But both owed to Byzantium all the elements of their greatness.

So it was that, in the tenth century, the Byzantine Empire was truly the universal empire, whose influence and ambition extended over nearly the whole of the civilized world. Its internal organization, as it appears at that time, afforded an equally solid foundation for its power and its prestige.

The Government of the Empire.—The Greek emperor — the *Basileus*, as he was officially styled — was, in truth, a very great personage. Heir of the Roman Cæsars, he, like them, was at once the supreme head of the army and the living voice of the law. Through his relations with the Oriental monarchies, he became the all-powerful master (*despot, autocrator*), the emperor *par excellence*, the rival and successor of the Great King. Christianity had given him additional sanctity and prestige. The elect of God, set apart by the consecration of a divine investiture, vicar and representative of God on earth, he partook, in some sort, of his divinity. In the ceremonial of the Court; in the complications of its etiquette, magnificent, and at the same time a bit puerile, whose rites Constantine Porphyrogenitus amused himself by codifying in the "Book of Ceremonies"; in all the manifestations of that policy of ostentation and magnificence by which Byzantium had always boasted of astonishing and dazzling the barbarians, the emperor appeared as a superhuman being. And so, whatever touched his person was declared to be "sacred," and art encircled his head with the halo, as it did those of the divine persons and the saints.

Sovereign by divine right, absolute and despotic, the emperor held in his own hands all authority; and it is easy to see how much the Empire gained by this unity of direction, when it was a strong hand that held the reins; and it often was. In the Byzantine constitution there was no balance to this supreme power. The Senate was no more than a council of state, composed of docile high functionaries; the people was only a plebeian multitude, often turbulent and factious, which had to be fed and amused. The Church, notwithstanding the high position she held in the Byzantine social hierarchy, notwithstanding the danger due to her wealth and ambition, was more submissive than ever to the State after the close of the Iconoclastic Controversy. The army alone was a power which had often made itself manifest by military uprisings and revolutions. Without wholly averting the peril from this quarter, the progress of the idea of legitimacy rendered it less frequent and less dangerous to the dynasty.

Byzantine Government and its Achievement.—This despotic government, no less absolute and infallible in the spiritual than in the temporal domain, was served by a trained administrative hierarchy, strongly centralized and under admirable discipline. In the capital, surrounding the prince, the ministers, who were the heads of the chief departments, directed the State from above, and transmitted throughout the monarchy the will of the master. Innumerable bureaus worked under their orders, where the details of public affairs were studied, and decisions were prepared. As Rome did in the old days, Byzantium governed the world by the strong organization of its bureaucracy. In the provinces, where the system of *themes* had become the sole base of the administrative organization (there were thirty *themes* in the middle of the tenth century, eighteen in Asia and twelve in Europe), all authority was concentrated in the hands of an all-powerful personage, the *strategos*, appointed directly by the emperor, and responsible directly to him. Thus, from the top to the bottom of the administrative ladder, the whole personnel, being well recruited, well trained, wholly devoted to its task and encouraged to give good service by the advancement vouchsafed by the prince in the shrewdly devised system of offices and dignities, acquitted itself with far-sighted zeal of the double rôle assigned to it by the emperor.

The first task of the administration was to supply the government with money—a difficult task; for in Byzantium the receipts of the treasury and the innumerable outlays caused by the imperial policies and magnificence never balanced; the grandiose projects and the insufficient resources were always out of proportion to each other.

The other task of the imperial government was, perhaps, still more difficult. The Byzantine monarchy had neither unity of race nor unity of language. It was, as someone has said, "an artificial creation, governing twenty different nationalities, and binding them together with this formula: one master, one faith." It was the admirable achievement of the government to give to this state with no nationality the necessary cohesion and unity, by the common imprint of Hellenism and by the common profession of the orthodox faith. Greek was the language of the government, of the Church, and of society. It assumed in the cosmopolitan Empire the false aspect, as it were, of a national language. By its skill in propagating Greek culture, by the deft art which it brought to bear in managing and assimilating the conquered peoples, the imperial administration placed a common stamp upon the discordant elements that formed the monarchy; and there is no stronger testimony to the Empire's vitality and power of expansion. By the propagation of the orthodox faith, by the shrewd way in which it used the Church to effect a moral conquest of the countries subdued by force, the government succeeded in bringing together and fusing the diverse races ruled by the *Basileus*. It was, in very truth, the stout armor that upheld the monarchy and made of it a strong and homogeneous body.

Legislation.—The emperors of the Macedonian line strove to strengthen this cohesion even more by a great legislative undertaking: they restored the ancient body of law created by Justinian, adapting it to the new conditions of social life. Basil I took the initiative in this great enterprise, by collecting in the *Prochiros Nomos* (879), the most important portions of the *Corpus Juris Civilis*, and by having prepared, under the title of *Epanagoge* (886), a manual of customary law. His son, Leo VI, completed the work by having published, under the title of *Basilica* (887–

893), a complete code of sixty books, a compilation and summary of juridical works promulgated during the reign of Justinian. The successors of the first two Macedonian emperors showed an equally great legislative activity, which, under Constantine Monomachus, was consummated by the foundation, in 1045, of the law school of Constantinople, destined to be a nursery for both jurists and public officials. Thus was the unity of the Empire placed upon a firm foundation.

Military Organization.—The power and prestige of the Empire were further augmented by an excellent army, admirably trained on scientific tactical principles, and which found in religious zeal and patriotic sentiment powerful motives for gallantry and enthusiasm; by a fine fleet, whose victories had given Byzantium the mastery of the sea, and which was, says an eleventh-century writer, "the glory of the Romans." For these troops, whom they regarded as the most valuable servitors of the monarchy, the great military emperors of the Macedonian dynasty had a constant and watchful solicitude; they determined that they should be assured every privilege and all possible consideration; that lands should be allotted to them and their heirs; and that they should receive the homage due to the defenders of the Empire and of Christendom. And the wonderful epic of the wars in Asia, the untiring ruthlessness of the struggle with the Bulgarians, showed what could be expected from those incomparable troops, inured to the profession of arms, and capable of sustaining suffering, fatigue, and privation in any degree. It is true that these forces consisted in great part of mercenaries, and they had all the shortcomings of armies of hirelings; nevertheless, under the illustrious officers who led them, they rendered brilliant service to the monarchy and adorned its banners with a halo of glory.

Economic Prosperity.—Wise financial administration and a wonderful development of industry and commerce bestowed wealth upon the Empire, together with added power. It has been calculated that the revenues of the monarchy in the eleventh century amounted to 650,000,000 francs, which would be the equivalent of more than three billions to-day; and at the death of Basil II, there was in the treasury a reserve of 220,000,000—more than a billion of our money. Despite the minute, inquisitorial regulations which the State imposed upon industry (Constantinople was, as someone has said, the paradise of monopoly and protectionism), the masterpieces that came from the hands of Byzantine artisans,— silk fabrics in brilliant colors, and heavy with embroidery; superb goldsmithery embellished with glistening enamel; dazzling jewels of precious stones and pearls; beautifully carved works of ivory; bronzes inlaid with silver; glassware embossed with gold,— all these marvels of an industry *de luxe* gave to the workshops of Greece extraordinary prestige throughout the world.

Despite the mistaken economic policy of the Empire, and the extremely vexatious system which it imposed upon business, the development of commerce was none the less remarkable. Through the activity of its merchants, the power of its navy, and the centres of exchange offered by its ports and its great markets, Byzantium monopolized the wealth of the whole world. Because of her position between the East and the West, at the outlet of all the routes of world-commerce, Constantinople was the great warehouse where all nations gathered, where all the products of the universe were exchanged. It has been estimated that, in the capital alone, the receipts from traders' royalties and from customs brought into the treasury annually 7,300,000 *sous* in gold—equivalent to more than 500,000,000 to-day.[1]

Distinction in Arts and Letters.—This development of industrial and commercial life was accompanied by a similar enlargement of intellectual life. In the rehabilitated University of Constantinople, eminent teachers, under the solicitous patronage of the sovereign, taught philosophy, rhetoric, and the sciences; and around their chairs students crowded, coming from all points of the Byzantine and Arabian Orient. On emerging from the Iconoclastic Controversy, at the touch of rediscovered antiquity, a new birth took place in all the domains of thought, and the emperors themselves did not disdain to become authors.

On the initiative of Constantine (VII) Porphyrogenitus, the tenth century made an inventory of the riches which the past had bequeathed to it. It was the age of encyclopædias of history, of law, of administration, of grammar, of science, of hagiography. Upon

[1] 1920

these bases original thought rested, to take breath for a further advance. The epoch of the Macedonian emperors witnessed the rise to eminence, in the ninth century, of a Photius, prodigious scholar, fearless and powerful intellect; in the eleventh century, of a Psellus, universal genius, the most inquisitive, brilliant, and original intellect of his time, who restored the Platonic philosophy to its place of honor, and by virtue of his talent as a writer, deserves to be placed on a par with the greatest. About them was a constellation of notable men—historians like Constantine Porphyrogenitus, Leo the Deacon, and Michael Attaleiates; chroniclers like Simeon Magistros and Scylitzes; philosophers, theologians, and poets. Beside this scholarly and worldly literature, popular poetry played its part, and the epic of Digenis Acritas, comparable to the Song of Roland or to the romance of the Cid, gave a new and unfamiliar impulse to Byzantine scholarship.

In art also the epoch of the Macedonian emperors marked a new golden age. Basil I and his successors were, like Justinian, great builders; and the architects they employed, with an ingenious and creative fancy, reproduced in a succession of charming churches the type created in St. Sophia. So that the art of this period, like its literature, was entirely governed by the influence of the revivified ancient and profane tradition. Byzantium returned to Hellenistic conceptions, to simplified dispositions, to sculptural attitudes, in which the more intimate knowledge of the Mussulman Orient blended the taste for sumptuous and refined ornamentation with the striving for brilliant coloring.

Side by side with the religious art there appears a profane art, for the behoof of the emperor and grandees, deriving its inspiration from classical history and mythology, and finding expression in *genre* subjects and in historical paintings and portraits. In the decoration of the churches, as in that of the palaces, there is manifest a fondness for ostentation and amazing magnificence. Mosaics like those in the convent of St. Luke—above all, like those of Daphni, the masterpiece of Byzantine art; or those of St. Sophia at Kiev, which attest the immense influence that this art exerted throughout the East; wonderful manuscripts, illuminated for the emperors, like the Gregory Nazianzen, the Psalter in the Bibliothèque Nationale at Paris, the Basilian Menologion in the Vatican, and the Psalter in the Library of St. Marks at Venice; dazzling enamels, like the reliquary of Limburg, and the Icons representing St. Michael, preserved in the treasury of St. Marks; the ivories, too, and the rich fabrics suffice to show what masterpieces Byzantine art was capable of creating at that time. It created something even more remarkable—the skilful disposition of the decorations, which made paintings a means of instruction in the service of the Church; and that new iconography, so varied and so rich, which corresponds to the renaissance of the ninth century. And by all these means, Byzantine art exerted its influence potently throughout the world, in Bulgaria as in Russia, in Armenia as in Southern Italy.

Constantinople was the resplendent source of this marvelous harvest, the queen of refinement, the capital of the civilized world. Behind the stout walls that defended it, the city "guarded by God" contained incomparable splendors: St. Sophia, whose harmonious beauty and sumptuous ceremonial struck dumb with wonder all who visited it; the Sacred Palace, whose indescribable magnificence ten generations of emperors had made it their proud duty to augment; the Hippodrome, where the government brought together all the spectacles that could amuse the populace—these were the three centres around which gravitated all Byzantine life.

Beside these was a multitude of churches and monasteries, the splendors of the palaces, the wealth of the bazaars, the masterpieces of ancient art, filling the squares and the streets, and making of the city the most admirable of museums. In the tenth century, Constantinople alone boasted of possessing seven wonders,—as many as the whole ancient world had known in an earlier day,—"with which she adorned herself," according to one writer, "as with so many stars." Strangers, in the East and the West alike, dreamed of Byzantium as of a city unique in the world, resplendent in a shimmering of gold. Among the Slavs as among the Arabs, in Italy as in distant France, the obsession of Byzantium and the influence which its civilization exercised were deep-rooted; the Greek monarchy, under the Macedonian emperors, was one of the most powerful states in existence; but while it excited admiration, it also excited universal cupidity—a serious menace for the future.

IV. CAUSES OF THE EMPIRE'S WEAKNESS

OTHER more imminent perils threatened the continuance of this prosperity.

The Social Question and Feudal Revolts.—At the end of the ninth century, and throughout the tenth, a formidable social question perturbed the Byzantine Empire. Two classes were face to face—the poor (πένητες) and the powerful (δυνατοί); and through the incessant encroachments of the latter upon the property and liberty of the former, little by little a great feudal aristocracy had grown up within the Empire,—especially in the Asiatic provinces,—possessed of vast domains, dependents, and vassals, whose influence was still further augmented by the high administrative offices which it held, and by the military commands which placed the army in its hands. Rich, powerful, popular, this nobility was a political as well as a social menace to the government.

The emperors realized this, and fought with all their might against these undisciplined barons, who flattered themselves that they could impose their will on the *Basileus*, and who, at all events, by the immunities they claimed, diminished the resources of the treasury, and, by usurping the military fiefs allotted to the soldiers, dried up one of the most fruitful sources of recruitment of the army.

Basil I, in this as in everything else, inaugurated the policy of the dynasty, and endeavored to limit the encroachments of the nobles. His successors carried on his work. A series of decrees promulgated by Romanus

(I) Lecapenus (922–934), by Constantine VII (947), by Romanus II, and by Nicephorus Phocas, had for their object to ensure protection to small holdings, and to prevent the feudal nobles "from swallowing the possessions of the poor." The constant renewal of these measures proves that the danger was constantly increasing. The events of the second half of the tenth century were to show this in striking fashion.

Soon after the assassination of Nicephorus Phocas, the first feudal uprising took place in Asia Minor (971), under the leadership of Bardas Phocas, a nephew of the late Emperor. The insurrection was not suppressed without difficulty. It broke out again, even more formidable, during the first years of the reign of Basil II. In 976, a veritable Asiatic *Fronde* made its appearance. Bardas Sclerus, a great feudal lord, took the lead in it, and, gathering about him all the dis-affected, all the adventurers, all those who hoped to gain something in a revolution, he made himself, in a few weeks, the master of Asia, and threatened Con-stantinople (978).

The government appealed to another feudal lord for help against this feudal pretender. Bardas Phocas defeated Sclerus on the field of Pankalia (979), and crushed the insurrection. But a new revolt broke out when the more firmly established power of Basil II seemed to threaten the aristocracy. Phocas and Scle-rus, the foes of yesterday, became reconciled, to rise against the Emperor (987). The remarkable vigor of Basil II triumphed everywhere, Phocas, beaten at Chrysopolis, opposite Constantinople, to which he had already laid siege (988), was killed on the field of

Abydos (989); Sclerus was compelled to submit. But the Emperor never forgot these feudal insurrections, and in the decree of 996 he struck at the great usurping barons with savage ferocity. It seemed that the crown had taken a decisive revenge upon the feudal rebels of Anatolia.

But in fact, all these measures proved unavailing. The government endeavored in vain to restrain the development of great estates, to crush the barons with taxes, to lessen their influence over the army: nothing was accomplished. The feudal aristocracy was destined to triumph over the imperial power; and in the weakness and anarchy which marked the second half of the eleventh century, it was a feudal family, that of the Comneni, which ensured the salvation of the monarchy.

The Religious Aristocracy.—Side by side with lay feudalism, religious feudalism was neither less powerful, nor less dangerous.

In the tenth century, as in the eighth, an important part of all landed property was immobilized in the hands of the monks, to the great detriment of the treasury and the army. The emperors of the tenth century endeavored to restrain the increase of the monastic holdings: in 964, Nicephorus Phocas even went so far as to forbid the founding of a new convent, or any donation to existing monasteries. But, in the Byzantine Empire, the Church was too powerful for such measures to be kept long in force, and the Empire needed the aid of the Church too often, not to handle her gently. In 988, Basil I abrogated the decree of Phocas. The monastic party had won.

Nor, when confronted by the secular clergy, did the emperor always have the last word. By virtue of the extent of his jurisdiction, of his prominent position in the Church, of the army of monks in his obedience, of the influence he exerted, and of the vast ambition his power awoke in him, the Patriarch of Constantinople was a formidable personage. If a patriarch devoted to the government was able to render signal service, a hostile patriarch was peculiarly dangerous, and his opposition might hold the emperor himself in check. Leo VI learned this in his last controversy with the Patriarch Nicholas; although he finally compelled the prelate to abdicate (907), nevertheless, after the Emperor's death, he resumed his seat (912); during the minority of Constantine VII, he was ruling minister, and played a decisive part in the internal revolutions of the Empire as well as in the guidance of its foreign policy; and the *tomus unionis* (920), in which was adjudicated the question of fourth marriages, which had formerly set the patriarch at odds with the emperor, was an outstanding triumph for him.

The Patriarch Polyeuctes, too, defied Nicephorus Phocas; and although he eventually had to submit, none the less he forced Tzimisces (970) to revoke all the measures unfavorable to the Church. But the ambition of the patriarchs of Constantinople was to have even more serious results: it was to lead to the rupture with Rome, and the schism between the two churches.

Once before, as we know, the ambition of Photius had brought about such a rupture. The accession of

Basil I inaugurated a different religious policy; the Patriarch was dispossessed, and the Œcumenical Council, held at Constantinople in 869, renewed the union with Rome. Photius, however, was restored to his seat in 877; again, at the Council of 879, he broke with the Papacy; and even though he fell finally in 886, and the union was solemnly renewed in 893, the latent conflict still existed between the two churches, less, to be sure, on account of the secondary questions of dogma and discipline which separated them, than because of the obstinate refusal of the Greeks to accept the Roman primacy, and because of the ambition of the patriarchs of Constantinople to be popes of the East. From the end of the tenth century the hostility was very bitter; in the middle of the eleventh century, the ambition of Michael Ceroularius was all that was needed to make the rupture complete.

V. DECADENCE OF THE EMPIRE IN THE ELEVENTH CENTURY (1025–1081)

NOTWITHSTANDING the real perils that threatened the Empire, its prestige and power might have been maintained by vigorous rulers, carrying on the tradition of a wise and resolute scheme of government. Unluckily, there was a succession of reigns of women, of commonplace and neglectful sovereigns; and this condition of affairs was the starting-point of a new disaster.

The deterioration began on the death of Basil II, under his brother, Constantine VIII (1025–1028), and progressed under the latter's daughters: first, Zoë, and the three husbands—Romanus III (1028–1034),

Michael IV (1034–1041), and Constantine (IX) Monomachus (1042–1054)—with whom she shared the
throne (she died in 1050); then, Theodora (1054–
1056). It became even more flagrantly manifest after
the close of the Macedonian dynasty. A military *coup
d'état* placed Isaac Comnenus on the throne (1057–
1059); his abdication brought about the elevation of
Constantine (X) Ducas (1059–1067). Then came Romanus (IV) Diogenes (1067–1071), who was deposed
by Michael (VII) Ducas (1071–1078); a fresh revolution gave the crown to Nicephorus Botaniates (1078–
1081). During these brief reigns, anarchy continued
to increase, and the formidable straits in which the
Empire was involved, without and within, grew more
and more difficult.

Normans and Turks.—Byzantium was now falling
back on all her frontiers. On the Danube, the Petchenegs, nomads of Turkish race, crossed the river and
occupied the country as far as the Balkans. Western Bulgaria revolted (1040), under the leadership
of Peter Delcanus, descendant of Tsar Samuel;
Thessalonica was threatened by the rebels, and although the uprising was finally put down, the country,
smarting under the tyranny of Byzantium, remained
all ready to secede. Even Serbia revolted and demanded her independence. In the Adriatic, Venice
appropriated the heritage of the Empire. But two adversaries were especially to be dreaded—the Normans
in Europe and the Seljuk Turks in Asia.

Settled in Southern Italy about the middle of the
eleventh century, and supported by the Papacy, the

Normans, under the leadership of Robert Guiscard, took from the Greek Empire, bit by bit, all that it still possessed in the peninsula. In vain did George Maniakes, the Byzantine Governor of Italy, after notable victories over the Arabs of Sicily (1038–1040), arrest for a moment the progress of the Normans (1042). When he was no more, everything collapsed: Troja fell in 1060, Otranto in 1068, Bari, the last Byzantine stronghold, submitted in 1071. Soon the ambition of the Duke of Apulia extended to the other shore of the Adriatic; he built a navy, and prepared to intervene in Illyria. In 1081, his son Bohemond landed on the coast of Epirus, and Guiscard, with 30,000 men, made ready to follow him.

In Asia, the situation was similar. Led by three noteworthy men,—Toghrul Beg, Alp Arslan (1065–1072), and Malek Shah (1072–1092),—the Seljuk Turks attacked the Empire. At first, they were thrown back by the solid line of fortresses built by Basil II. But Armenia, loosely held by Byzantium, and disaffected because of the religious persecutions to which she was exposed, was of uncertain fidelity. In 1064, the Turks took Ani, and, soon afterward, Cæsarea and Chones. In vain did the energetic Romanus (IV) Diogenes try to check their progress: he was defeated at Manzikiert (1071), north of the Lake of Van, and fell into the hands of the infidels.

Byzantium never recovered completely from this great disaster. Thereafter, all the eastern part of Asia Minor, Armenia, Cappadocia, all those regions from which the Empire recruited its best soldiers, its most renowned generals, were irrevocably lost. Thereafter, in the growing anarchy throughout the Empire, the Turks had things their own way: Iconium fell into their hands; then Nicæa, whither the Byzantines themselves summoned them; and in 1079 they took possession of Chrysopolis, just opposite Constantinople.

Does this mean that the Normans and Turks were more redoubtable adversaries than so many others whom Byzantium had formerly vanquished? No; but the Empire was weaker. All the perils that were impending in the tenth century had carried out their threats.

Schism and Internal Anarchy.—In 1054, the ambition of the Patriarch Michael Ceroularius precipitated a serious conflict. He had attacked Rome when she claimed to have reëstablished her authority over the churches of Southern Italy. Pope Leo IX retaliated with equal vigor, and the papal legates sent to Constantinople outraged Byzantine pride by their arrogant attitude. They came very soon to the breaking point. The legates solemnly excommunicated the Patriarch. Ceroularius, by rebelling, forced upon the Emperor Constantine (IX) Monomachus the schism he desired. The separation of the two churches was accomplished.

This rupture with the Papacy was to have very grave consequences for the Empire. Not only did it hasten the fall of Greek domination in Italy, but, what was still more important, it made an abyss between Byzantium and the West which nothing could fill. In the eyes of the Latins the Greeks were thenceforth no more than schismatics, to whom they owed neither consideration nor tolerance, and whom they had the strongest reasons to distrust. On the other hand, the Byzantines obstinately persisted in their rancorous hatred of Rome. Thereafter the question of the relations between the Papacy and the orthodox Church bore heavily upon the destinies of the monarchy.

Finally, within the Empire, the circumstances which had brought about the schism exhibited, in striking fashion, the weakness of the imperial power against the all-powerful patriarch; Michael Ceroularius was not likely to forget it.

But, above all, the feudal peril was becoming more threatening day by day. In order to crush the too powerful aristocracy, the government deemed it a clever move to combat the army, upon which the feudal lords relied, and whose strength was making itself ominously manifest at that very time, by uprisings like that of George Maniakes, the hero of the wars in Sicily and Italy (1043), or that of Leo Tornikius (1047). A civilian party was formed, whose task it was to prove to the troops that they were under suspicion. The reign of Constantine Monomachus saw the first triumph of this party. Under that Emperor, pleasure-seeking and unwarlike, the army was notably weakened: more generally than ever the national troops were replaced by mercenaries,—Normans, Scandinavians, Russians, Anglo-Saxons,—in whom it was believed that more confidence could be placed. The military budget was pared down, the fortresses were neglected, generals were put aside or dismissed. The

government was in the hands of men of letters—
Psellus, Xiphilin, John Mauropus, and the like. The
foundation of the law school was intended mainly to
provide the government with civil servants.

A conflict soon became inevitable between this all-
powerful bureaucracy, supported by the Senate, and
the army. It was violent when it came. In 1057, a
proclamation, which the Patriarch Ceroularius approved, placed Isaac Comnenus, an illustrious general, on the throne. But when Isaac, losing heart, ab-
dicated, in 1059, the accession of the Ducases marked
a reaction against the military party, and assured
anew, and more amply than ever, the triumph of the
bureaucracy. Romanus Diogenes restored for a time
the power of the army. He succumbed under the fierce
attack of the coalition of his opponents; and the
reign of Michael VII, whose first prime minister was
Psellus, seemed the definitive triumph of the civilian
party.

All this had important consequences. Externally,
the boundaries of the Empire were receding on all
sides; the peoples, inadequately defended by a too
feeble government, and, moreover, ground down by
taxes, separated from Byzantium, and, as in the last
days of the Roman Empire, called in the barbarians.
At home, amid the universal anarchy, the feudal aristocracy lifted its head; the army, malcontent because
of the hostility shown it, was ripe for insurrection.
Even the mercenaries rebelled, and the Norman *con-
dottieri* in the service of the Empire—Hervé, Robert
Crepin, Roussel of Bailleul—worked solely for their
own interest. Revolution succeeded revolution. Ni-

cephorus Botaniates rose in Asia against Michael VII; at the same time Nicephorus Bryennius revolted in Europe (1078). Then, when Nicephorus Botaniates became Emperor (1078–1081), other pretenders, Basilakes and Melissenus, rose against him. The Empire, invaded, exhausted, disaffected, clamored loudly for a savior.

He appeared in the person of Alexius Comnenus, the best general of the Empire. The *coup d'état* that placed him on the throne (April first, 1081), by putting an end to thirty years of anarchy, marked the triumph of the feudal aristocracy and the army over the civilian party, and of the provinces over the capital. But it was to give the Empire a new period of greatness.

CHAPTER VI

The Comnenus Dynasty, 1081-1204

I. THE SOVEREIGNS OF THE DYNASTY OF THE COMNENI

LIKE the Capets in France, the Comneni were a great feudal family, and their accession seemed to set a seal upon the triumph of the military aristocracy. Like the Capets, the Comneni were able to reëstablish the enfeebled imperial authority, to rehabilitate the Empire, exhausted by thirty-one years of anarchy, and, despite overwhelming difficulties, to give it yet another century of grandeur and glory.

Of course, the times were too difficult, the situation too critical, for the Comneni to be able to restore to Byzantium all her aforetime brilliancy and prosperity. The Turks were at Iconium and remained there; in the Balkans, with the support of expanding Hungary, the Slavic nations were setting up states that were almost independent; and lastly, in the West ominous clouds were gathering, because of the overweening and unseasonable aims of Byzantine imperialism, the political ambition born of the Crusades, and the grasping economic cupidity of Venice. Nevertheless, the Comneni shed a final ray of glory on the Empire, and, amid the distress of the following centuries, the people very often recalled the epoch of the Comneni as preëminently brilliant and blest.

Descended from a great aristocratic and military family, the emperors of the Comnenus line were, first of all, soldiers. But they were something more. Alexius, founder of the dynasty (1081–1118), was an intelligent man, most astute and determined; a great general, shrewd diplomat, and excellent administrator, he came forward, at the critical period of the monarchy, as the man of the hour. And, in fact, he was able to hold in check enemies outside the Empire, and to reëstablish law and order within.

John, his son and successor (1118–1142), had no less eminent qualities. Brought up strictly, of rigid morals, a sworn foe of luxury and dissipation, of a gentle and generous disposition and keen intelligence, he merited by his lofty moral character the surname of Kalo-John (John the Good). Being very brave, and eager for military renown, he was thoroughly aware of the importance of his profession of king, and his political ideals were on a very high plane. His father had defended the frontiers; he dreamed of extending them, of reconquering for the monarchy its lost provinces, and of restoring its ancient splendor.

Manuel (1143–1180), son of John, was the most attractive of the Comneni. Intelligent, lovable, generous, he was at the same time a Byzantine *basileus*, educated and cultivated,—even a theologian,—and a Western cavalier. Of noteworthy physical courage, he had more inclination to Western customs than any other Greek sovereign; and the Latins, whom he resembled in so many ways, admired him more than any other emperor. He was devoted to luxurious living and pleasure, and filled the twelfth century with the fame of his adventures. A great politician, too, and most ambitious, he included the whole of the Europe of his time within the purview of his imperial policy, which was often unreasonable and utopian in its aims. But, although he exhausted the realm and brought it to the verge of destruction by the extraordinary effort that he required it to put forth, he was, none the less, by virtue of the far-reaching scope of his projects, and his persistent struggle to carry them out, perhaps the last of the great sovereigns who sat upon the imperial throne.

Andronicus (1183–1185), the last and most exceptional of the Comneni, combined with most admirable gifts of political insight and gallantry in war, and the rarest qualities of refinement and charm, a spirit of intrigue and adventure, a lack of scruple and of moral sense, and a cruelty, often unspeakable, which make him, on the whole, one of the most typical figures of the Byzantine Empire. After filling the twelfth century with the noise of romantic adventures and the scandal of his manner of life, once seated on the throne, he compelled his contemporaries to believe that, because of his great ability, "he might have been equal to the greatest." He might have been the savior and regenerator of the Empire, but he only accelerated its fall. Less than twenty years after his death,— twenty years of anarchy,— Constantinople was taken by the Latins (1204), and the Empire rehabilitated by the Comneni went to pieces.

BYZANTINE EMPIRE

The Balkan Policy.— At the end of the eleventh century, the power of the Empire was seriously impaired in the Balkans. The discontented Slavic vassals began to secede from Byzantium. Since 1076 Croatia had been an independent kingdom; Serbia, which had again rebelled in 1071, accepted the Greek suzerainty with reluctance; Danubian Bulgaria was occupied by the Petchenegs, and Western Bulgaria was restive under the Byzantine yoke. In Thrace there was disquieting religious opposition: the Bogomil heresy, which had developed tremendously since the tenth century in a country inhabited wholly by Paulicians, afforded, as always, a pretext for race-antagonism to manifest itself at Byzantium. But, above all, beyond the Danube, expanding Hungary aspired to play a prominent rôle, and to take its place in Balkan affairs, to the prejudice of the Empire.

In 1084, the heretics in Thrace revolted, and called the Petchenegs to their aid. On two occasions (1086 and 1088) the barbarian hordes crushed the Greek armies, and the latter were forced to sue for peace (1089). But the Petchenegs soon came back. This time Alexius Comnenus inflicted a severe defeat upon them on the banks of the Leburnion (1091)—a defeat so complete, that for a generation one might have believed that they were exterminated. Nevertheless, in 1121 they reappeared. John Comnenus thereupon defeated them again (1122). Thenceforth, the Petchenegs disappear from history. But for many a year afterward the Byzantines remembered them, and solemnly celebrated the anniversary of the day that witnessed their downfall.

This was merely an episode. Serbia was more threatening. Constantine Bodin had subdued the districts of Dioclea, Bosnia, and Rascia, and had founded a homogeneous state which Alexius Comnenus was unable to subjugate (1091–1094). Fortunately for the Byzantines, anarchy very soon disrupted the young kingdom. John Comnenus profited by this to bring a part of the district again under Greek vassalage; but Rascia remained independent; it was destined to become the centre of the national resistance and the starting-point of the reconstruction of the state. However, to arrest the progress of Hungary, which was stretching out in the direction of Croatia, Bosnia, and Dalmatia, and was making its influence felt in Serbia, the Empire, in conformity with the timeworn methods of its diplomacy, strove to set up in Serbia a prince devoted to its interest.

Lying between the German Empire and the Byzantine Empire, Hungary was an important pawn on the European chessboard. The sovereigns of Constantinople endeavored to take it. John Comnenus intervened in the Hungarian quarrels, in support of the blind Bela, son of the dethroned King Koloman; and although he did not succeed in restoring him, he did, at all events, by the peace of 1126, gain possession of the invaluable bridgehead of Branitzova.

Manuel Comnenus displayed even more energy in arresting the encroachments of Hungary, and in rescuing the Slavic states from her yoke. He brought the Serbs once more under Greek suzerainty (1151), and gave them for their ruler Stephen Nemanya (1163), who proved himself, despite a few escapades, a faithful and submissive vassal, at least during the lifetime of the Emperor. He whipped the Hungarians in a succession of victorious campaigns (1152–1154), and in 1156 forced upon them a peace advantageous to the Empire. Moreover, when King Geisa II died, Manuel intervened in the war of the succession which followed, and gave his support against Stephen III to the young Bela, whom he even thought of making his son-in-law.

But Hungary was looking more and more in the direction of Germany. Thereupon Manuel renewed the war (1165). Zeugmin and Sirmium fell into the hands of the Greeks; Dalmatia, lost long before, was reconquered; the victory of Zeugmin (1167) finally obliged Hungary to make peace (1168). By this peace, the Empire gained Dalmatia and part of Croatia. Some years later, Manuel's protégé ascended the throne of St. Stephen. Bela III (1173–1196) was, like Stephen Nemanya in Serbia, the vassal of Byzantium as long as the Emperor lived. These were important results, but, unfortunately, they were destined to be ephemeral.

Oriental Policy.—Asia, even more than the Balkans, engaged the attention of the Comneni. The continued successes of the Seljuk Turks had gradually driven the Greeks from almost the entire Orient. Soliman, a Turkish emir, reigned at Cyzicus and Nicæa, and Alexius Comnenus, harassed by other, more urgent cares, was forced to recognize his conquests (1082). In

1085, Antioch fell into the hands of the infidels. At Smyrna, the Emir Tzachas (1089–1090) built a fleet and threatened Constantinople. Fortunately for Byzantium, the death of Malek Shah (1092) led to the dismemberment of the Seljuk Empire. The Greeks took advantage of this to regain a foothold in Bithynia, and the new Sultan of Iconium, Kilij Arslan I (1092–1106), had to consent to peace.

Alexius Comnenus derived no less profit from the first Crusade. The capture of Nicæa by the Latins (1097) enabled him to reconquer a considerable part of the coast of Anatolia, Smyrna, Ephesus, and so forth; and, although the Emperor was soon at odds with the Crusaders, he shrewdly turned to his own advantage the embarrassment they caused the infidels. In addition, the death of Kilij Arslan had greatly weakened the Sultanate of Iconium. In 1116, the Emperor opened a vigorous offensive, and, as a result of the victory of Philomelion, he imposed peace on the Turks.

When the first of the Comneni died, the Empire possessed, in Anatolia, Trebizond and the whole coast of the Black Sea, all the littoral as far as the neighborhood of Antioch, and everything west of a line passing through Sinope, Gangra, Ancyra, Amorion, and Philomelion. In Asia, as in the Balkans, Alexius had gloriously restored the power of Byzantium.

John Comnenus gave even more attention to Asiatic affairs. He had a twofold purpose in the East: to carry the Byzantine frontier back as far as Antioch and the line of the Euphrates, and to compel the Armenian princes of Cilicia and the Latin states to which the Crusade had given birth in the East, to accept his suzerainty. Early in his reign (1119–1120) he reconquered the whole region lying between the valley of the Meander and Attalia, thus wiping out the inconvenient wedge which the Mussulman possessions inserted between the Byzantine territories in northern and southern Anatolia.

After 1130 he carried the war into Paphlagonia, and the Byzantine armies made their way to the banks of the Halys. Gangra and Kastamuni were retaken from the Turks (1134), and those long-lost regions were restored to the Empire. Later on, we shall see how the Emperor made his power felt in Cilicia and in Syria; how he appeared to the Armenian and Latin princes in the light of suzerain and commander, ready to lead them against the infidels. Down to the very end of his reign, the war against the Mussulmans and the reconquest of Asia were his chief preoccupation. In 1139 he led an expedition against Cæsarea; in 1142, on the eve of his death, he was planning to reconquer Syria.

At first, Manuel Comnenus continued his father's policy. In 1146, he advanced as far as the walls of Iconium. But the invasion of the Normans and the second Crusade forced him to direct his attention elsewhere (1147). Not until much later was he able to turn his eyes toward the Orient. But although, like his father, he dreamed of imposing his suzerainty upon the Armenian and Latin states, and succeeded in doing so, his policy regarding the Turks was more uncertain and feebler. About the middle of the twelfth century, it would have required only a slight exertion to destroy the Sultanate of Iconium and to reconquer all Asia as far as the Taurus. Manuel, carried away by the ambitious visions of his Western policy, could not put forth that exertion. He allowed himself to be taken in by the ostensible tokens of submission which the crafty Sultan of Iconium, Kilij Arslan II (1156–1192), freely offered him, and he imprudently allowed him to erect fortifications, to crush his rivals one after another, and to create a homogeneous and powerful state in the place of the small principalities whose rivalries had so well served the Empire. Instead of bestirring himself, Manuel for eleven years (1164–1175) confined himself to a purely defensive policy, simply fortifying his frontier; and when he finally realized the danger, and assumed the offensive, it was too late. In 1176, the imperial army sustained a terrible defeat at Myriocephalus. True, successful campaigns in Bithynia and in the valley of the Meander (1177) repaired in part the disastrous effect of this defeat. The Mussulmans were, none the less, at the end of Manuel's reign, far more powerful than they were at his accession. The Sultanate of Iconium had become a powerful state, and from 1174 on, Saladin reigned in Syria.

Western Policy. Normans and Venetians.—The fact is that, throughout the whole period of the Comneni, the closer relations between Byzantium and the West had given the Empire new matter for reflection, and had awakened far-reaching ambitions in those who governed it. The centre of gravity of Byzantine policy shifted, to the great prejudice and great peril of the monarchy.

Alexius Comnenus became emperor just as the Normans under Robert Guiscard were landing in Epirus (1081). The Emperor's diplomacy succeeded, by paying dear in other ways, in securing the alliance of Venice against them. But the imperial army was, nevertheless, severely defeated in the neighborhood of Durazzo (1081), which Guiscard soon seized. In the following year, Bohemond made electrifying progress in Epirus, Macedonia, and even in Thessaly. Larissa delayed him for six months, however; and little by little, thanks to the Emperor's tenacity, fortune changed sides. The Norman army, decimated by illness, weakened by the attacks of the Greeks, and still more disorganized by the imperial diplomacy, had to retreat. At sea, the Venetians destroyed the Norman fleet (1085). The death of Robert Guiscard (1085) finally rehabilitated the fortunes of Byzantium. The Norman peril was averted.

It was, however, destined soon to revive. In 1105, Bohemond, who had become Prince of Antioch, incited throughout the West a great crusade against the Greeks, and in 1107 he landed at Valona. The craft of Alexius triumphed once more over his adversary. In 1108, the Norman was obliged to sign a humiliating treaty, which placed him under the suzerainty of the Empire. It was a great triumph for Byzantium.

But, in the years that followed, the Norman kingdom of the Two Sicilies continued to increase in strength. Roger II was a source of anxiety to John Comnenus, who sought the support of Germany against him (1137). Ten years later, the rupture became flagrant. In 1147, the Norman fleet appeared in the Archipelago, ravaged Eubœa and Attica, pillaged Corinth and Thebes, and carried off to Palermo the workmen employed in the silk factories of these two great industrial towns. Manuel Comnenus, being occupied elsewhere, could make no headway at first against this invasion. But soon, thanks to the Venetian alliance, he recovered Corfu (1149), and carried the war into Italy, where he occupied Ancona (1151). Nevertheless, notwithstanding the death of Roger II (1154), and despite the powerful league which Byzantine diplomacy succeeded temporarily in forming against the King of Sicily, the Greeks had no success either on land or at sea. Manuel was compelled, in 1158, to sign an indecisive treaty with William I, which left the relations between the two states exceedingly strained. The trouble was that the West would not have at any price an Italy under Greek influence; and Venice in particular, the old ally of the Empire, was extraordinarily perturbed by it.

The Venetians had willingly supported the Greek Empire against the Norman at first; and in exchange for their support, they obtained from Alexius Comnenus large concessions for their commerce throughout the East (1082). But, notwithstanding these excellent political relations, the rapacity of the Venetian merchants soon made the Greeks uneasy. Alexius, to lessen somewhat the monopoly they enjoyed, granted like privileges to the Pisans (1111). John Comnenus refused to renew the treaty with Venice; and though, after four years of war (1122–1126), the Emperor was obliged to yield, nevertheless, like his father, he endeavored to neutralize Venetian influence by treating with Pisa (1136) and with Genoa (1143). Manuel, too, at first sought the aid of Venice against the Normans, and paid her with ample concessions (1148).

But the misunderstanding between the two states continued to increase. The arrogance and rapacity of the Venetians in the East exasperated the Greeks. On the other hand, the Republic viewed with uneasiness Manuel's ambition with respect to Italy; and when the Emperor occupied Ancona, when he conquered Dalmatia, Venice saw that her domination of the Adriatic was in danger. Thereafter, a rupture was inevitable. Manuel provoked it by causing the arrest of all Venetians settled within the Empire (1171); the Republic retorted by sending her fleets to occupy Chios and ravage the Archipelago, and by forming an alliance with the King of Sicily. Manuel yielded (1175): he restored the privileges of the Venetians. But, as with the Normans, relations continued to be strained and tense; and the day was at hand when the Normans and Venetians were to make their hostility to the Empire painfully evident.

The Greek Empire and the Crusaders.—The antagonism between the Greek Orient and the Latin Occident was intensified by the Crusades.

When the armies of the first Crusade appeared before the walls of Constantinople (1096), Alexius Comnenus, who had never solicited the support of the West except to ask for mercenaries, was greatly perturbed by an expedition whose significance he could

not understand, and of which his old enemy Bohemond was one of the leaders. But, despite the brutal
conduct of the Latins, despite the insolence, the
cupidity, and the ill-dissimulated ambition of the
great barons, the Emperor endeavored to come to an
understanding with them: being too weak to repulse
them, he tried to make use of them. He flattered himself that, by paying the price, he could enlist the Crusaders in the service of the Empire; that he could bind
them to him by an oath of homage and fidelity, and
could employ them to reconquer Asia for Byzantium.

At first, he seemed to be successful. After more or
less objections, the leaders of the Crusade, one by one,
took an oath of allegiance to Alexius (1097), and prom-
ised to return to him all the towns that had formerly
belonged to the Empire which they should capture
from the Turks. It was by virtue of this agreement
that Nicæa, when taken, was turned over to the
Greeks, and that, at the outset, a body of Byzantine
troops accompanied the Crusaders. But when, after
taking Antioch, the Crusaders, regardless of their
promises, gave the city to Bohemond (1098), and
when, afterward, they refused to wait for the Emperor before marching on Jerusalem (1099), the rupture was complete. Alexius could not pardon Bohemond for his usurpation; he got along little better
with the other Latins settled in Syria. The failure of
the Crusade of 1101, for which the West held the
Greeks responsible, aggravated the misunderstanding. The failure of Bohemond's enterprise against the
Empire (1107) exasperated the ill-feeling of the Latins
for Byzantium. The Crusaders were really more to

blame than the Emperor; but rumors hostile to the Byzantines spread none the less throughout the West. An abyss yawned between the two powers.

The same thing happened at the beginning of the second Crusade (1147). Manuel, who was reigning at that time, was, like Alexius, greatly disturbed by the appearance under the walls of his capital of those vast armies, led by Conrad III, King of Germany, and Louis VII, King of France. With the Germans he almost came to an understanding, and got rid of them quickly; with the French, he had so much difficulty that at one time the Crusaders thought of taking Constantinople. Under these conditions, when the second Crusade came to its disastrous end, it was laid chiefly to the perfidy of the Greeks, whose rapacity had, in truth, been scandalous; and, in revenge for the failure of the expedition, the West thought for a moment of sending a crusade against Byzantium (1150). The fact is that the imperial policy with regard to the Latins of the Orient justified this distrust, and augmented the hostility between the two powers.

The Norman principality which the first Crusade set up at Antioch was most embarrassing to the Byzantines, because of the ambitions of its chiefs, Bohemond and Tancred. The Byzantines fought against it with all their resources, with arms and with diplomacy; for a time the treaty of 1108, which was forced upon Bohemond, seemed to assure the success of the imperial policy by placing Antioch under Greek suzerainty. But this treaty was never carried out. A new beginning had to be made. John and Manuel Comnenus applied themselves to the task, with even more far-reaching ambition. Both dreamed of actually establishing their authority over the Armenian principalities in Cilicia and the Latin states in Syria; and they succeeded in doing it.

About the year 1131, Leo, Prince of Armenia, added largely to his dominion at the expense of Greek Cilicia, and formed an alliance with his neighbors, the princes of Antioch, whom Byzantium had always regarded as rebellious vassals. John Comnenus seized the first opportunity to interfere. He subdued Cilicia (1137), compelled Raymond of Poitiers, Prince of Antioch, to do homage to him, and, assuming the rôle of a veritable suzerain in Frankish Syria, he led a great expedition against the Mussulmans (1138). However, he did not succeed in gaining possession of Antioch, as he wished. But his ambition did not abate. In 1142 he reappeared in Cilicia, to constitute there, in the Armenian states and Antioch, an appanage for his favorite son, Manuel. Death interrupted his plans (1143), and the Prince of Antioch seized the opportunity to take his revenge and recover his independence.

Manuel soon proved that he intended to continue his father's policy. Raymond, defeated, was fain to go to Constantinople to apologize, and to acknowledge himself a vassal of the Emperor (1145). A little later, in 1158, Manuel played his rôle of suzerain even more successfully. He conquered Cilicia, severely punished Renaud of Châtillon, Prince of Antioch, forced him to undergo a humiliating submission, and, escorted by all the Latin sovereigns of Syria, whose master he seemed to be, he made a solemn entry into Antioch.

Even the kings of Jerusalem were obliged to submit to Byzantine influence; we find them furnishing their quotas to the imperial army, marrying into the Comnenus family (Manuel, on his side, married a Latin princess, Mary of Antioch, in 1161), and pursuing, in concert with the Greeks, common enterprises against Egypt (1169). Byzantine civilization made its way into Frankish Syria, where Manuel's personal prestige was considerable.

Byzantine ambition was, apparently, realized. But, on the one hand, by exhausting the Latins in Syria, it had weakened their power to resist the infidels, and, above all, it had intensified the hatred of the West for Byzantium.

The Imperialistic Policy of the Comneni.—The far-reaching and ill-advised aims of Manuel's policy in the West finally brought the two powers face to face.

Like many of their predecessors, the Comneni dreamed of recovering their authority over Rome, whether by force or in concert with the Papacy, and of annihilating the Western Empire, which always seemed to them to have usurped their rights. Manuel Comnenus especially devoted himself to making these dreams a reality. We have seen how his successes over the Normans impelled him to intervene in the peninsula; how in Hungary, as well as in Italy, he pitted himself against the German Empire, where Frederic Barbarossa had reigned since 1152. It may be truly said that, in the mind of the Emperor, his western policy held the chief place; and that, throughout his reign, by divers means,—force of arms and diplomacy,

—he persistently pursued the ambitious goal that he had set before himself.

The break between Barbarossa and the Papacy (1158) offered him a pretext for drawing nearer to Rome. He took sides with Alexander III (1161); he dazzled the eyes of the Pontiff with the hope of re-uniting the Churches; he flattered himself that he might obtain from him in exchange the imperial crown of the West. At the same time, his diplomacy strove to conjure up enemies for Barbarossa, by en-couraging the Lombard League, and subsidizing Ancona, Genoa, Pisa, and Venice. And yet, while in-triguing in Italy and Germany, Manuel cherished visions of direct concert of action with the German Emperor.

No practical result came of these complicated and utopian schemes. The Pope could not consent to be-come a Byzantine bishop, in Rome as the capital of the reconstructed empire; the Italian republics were suspicious of Manuel's ambition; and, lastly, Barba-rossa, disgusted with Greek duplicity, became openly hostile and threatening (1177).

Thus the attraction of the West for Manuel Com-nenus was disastrous to the Empire. By his sympathy with the Latins, he irritated the Greeks; by his ambi-tion, he brought about a coalition of the West against Byzantium; by the incommensurable burden that his policy imposed upon the Empire, he exhausted it. In appearance, Manuel had bestowed upon the Empire incomparable renown in the world, and had made Constantinople the centre of European politics. In reality, when he died (1180), he left Byzantium ruined, exposed to the peril arising from the hatred of the Latins, and helpless in the face of the grave internal crisis that was imminent.

III. GOVERNMENT OF THE COMNENI, AND BYZANTINE CIVILIZATION IN THE TWELFTH CENTURY

THE first three Comneni were absorbed by the task of restoring to the imperial authority its former scope, and to the monarchy its former prosperity. They had made a great effort to reorganize the army, especially by introducing great numbers of mercenaries, many of whom came from the West; and, on the other hand, they had, not altogether wisely, neglected the navy, relying too much on the alliance with Venice, and the support of her fleets, to ensure their command of the sea. On the whole, however, they had succeeded in building up a formidable military force, capable both of defending the rehabilitated Empire and of maintaining the enhanced imperial authority. Alexius and John had, in equal degree, given close attention to the finances; and although the taxes were, to be sure, burdensome, and the tyranny of the treasury hard upon his subjects; although the reign of Manuel cost the Empire dear because of the expenditure necessitated by the wars, the diplomacy, and the luxurious tastes of the prince, nevertheless, in the twelfth century, the Greek Empire was wealthy, and its commercial prosperity genuine, despite the blunders of an economic policy which allowed foreigners imperceptibly to supplant the Greeks in the markets of the Orient; despite, too, the increasing rapacity of the commercial cities of

Italy, which exploited the Empire more and more for their own advantage, and were already setting up establishments there as in a conquered country.

The Comneni were most solicitous, too, concerning the affairs of the Church. They combatted with equal zeal heresy and free thought, when the latter showed itself in the University of Constantinople, through the renaissance of the Platonic philosophy. They were careful to oversee and reform the morals of the clergy, and especially to bring back to a simpler and more edifying manner of life the monks, for whom, at the end of the eleventh century, St. Christodulus, with the sanction of Alexius Comnenus, founded the model monastery of Patmos (1088). At Constantinople, they built many pious foundations,—convents, hospitals, churches,—of which the most noteworthy was that of the Pantocrator, erected by the Emperor John to be at once the centre of a great monastic and sanative institution, and the St. Denis of the dynasty.[1]

In fine, there have been few courts more magnificent or more refined than that of the Comneni. The palace of Blachernes, at the head of the Golden Horn, to which they moved their residence, was, as described by contemporaries, a marvel of splendor and beauty. There dwelt about the prince—especially in Manuel's day—a society enamoured of pleasure and merry-making, and which borrowed from the West some of its favorite diversions, as tournaments, joustings, and mystery plays; intrigue and amorous adventures played a large part there; women displayed their coquetry and charm; and all this youthful company,

[1] That is, its place of sepulture.

ardent and ebullient, was no less interested in the occult sciences, in magic and astrology, than in love with things of the spirit.

To attest the high degree of intellectual culture attained by Byzantium in the twelfth century, it is enough to recall the names of writers like Anna Comnena and Nicephorus Bryennius, Nicetas Acominatus and Eustathius of Thessalonica. A genuine renaissance of intellectual life and classical tradition took place; and the emperors deemed it an honor to patronize men of letters, scholars as well as theologians and official orators, whose eloquent harangues adorned all the great ceremonials, and court poets, like Theodore Prodromus, whose spirited talent expended itself in occasional poems, often amusing and clever. Art maintained no less gloriously the traditions of the preceding century; and its influence, extending from the heart of the East to the farthest limits of the West, made of Byzantium the educator of the universe and the queen of the civilized world.

In the Latin states of Syria, as well as in Venice and in Norman Sicily, churches and palaces were built, decorated in the Byzantine manner. Greek artists executed the mosaics of Bethlehem and Torcello, of the dome of Cefalu, of the Martorana, and of the Palatine Chapel at Palermo; and even to this day, the monument that gives the most exact picture of the splendors of Byzantium at that time is St. Mark's at Venice, with its five cupolas, the richness of its marbles and goldsmithery, its glistening mosaics, and the reflections of purple and gold with which it is all alight. Roman art itself borrowed from Byzantium certain features of its architecture and many of its decorative ideas.

By her wealth, by the beauty of her monuments, by the magnificence of her palaces, by the relics in her churches, Constantinople aroused the admiration of the whole world, and all those who visited the city returned home bedazzled. "She is the glory of Greece," said Odo of Deuil; "her wealth is far-famed, and she is even richer than she is reputed to be." "With the exception of Baghdad," writes Benjamin of Tudela, "there is no city in the universe to be compared with her." It is said, on the authority of Clari, that two thirds of the wealth of the world were at Constantinople, while the other third was distributed over the rest of the world. The Byzantine capital, according to one clever expression, was "the Paris of the Middle Ages." It was, according to Villehardouin, "the wealthiest city in the world," the city that was "sovereign over all others." An ominous prosperity, which excited envy as well as admiration, and which was destined to cost the monarchy dear, when the weakness of the Empire should become manifest to all eyes.

IV. THE BYZANTINE EMPIRE AT THE END OF THE TWELFTH CENTURY (1180–1204)

As long as Manuel Comnenus lived, his intelligence, energy, and ability assured good order at home, and maintained the prestige of Byzantium abroad. At his death, the whole edifice collapsed. As in the time of Justinian, so in the twelfth century, the imperial ambition envisaged projects too far-reaching. Their execution was difficult and disastrous. Involving the Empire too deeply in Western affairs, while pursuing the unwise visions of a grandiose imperialism, Manuel Comnenus, at one and the same time, was too heedless of the imminent peril in the Orient, and aroused the apprehension of the Latins, while he drained the monarchy dry. The hatred and rancor that he provoked, the rapacious greed that he permitted to burst into flame, were to have ominous consequences when the power fell into weaker hands.

Alexius II, son of Manuel, was a child; his mother, the regent Mary of Antioch, a Latin by birth, who relied upon the Latins for support, was unpopular. Andronicus Comnenus took advantage of the general discontent to make himself Emperor (1182–1185). The last of the Comneni might have been a great sovereign. He understood that the power of the feudal lords was a menace to the Empire, and he dealt severely with them; the insurrection of Isaac Angelus in Bithynia (1185) was drowned in blood. Andronicus reorganized the government, reduced expenses, lightened the taxes, and was well on the road to popularity, when external events—the Norman war, resulting in the capture of Thessalonica (1185), and the Hungarian war, resulting in the capture of Dalmatia—overthrew him. A revolution (1185) placed Isaac Angelus on the throne, and precipitated the downfall of the Empire. Isaac (1185–1195) had none of the qualities necessary to avert this threatening crisis. His brother Alexius III (1195–1203), who dethroned him, was equally worthless. The monarchy was ripe for destruction.

At home, the imperial power, weakened by this succession of revolutions and by incessant conspiracies, was singularly helpless. In the capital, the populace dictated the law to the government; in the provinces, the aristocracy raised its head once more, and the Empire fell apart. Isaac Comnenus proclaimed himself independent in Cyprus (1184), and Gabras at Trebizond; everywhere the great feudal families, the Cantacuzenes, Branas, Sguros, carved out for themselves lordships from the shreds of the monarchy. Disorder and destitution were everywhere: the burden of taxes was crushing, commerce was ruined, the treasury empty. Demoralization was rife, even in the Church, where the monks, breaking the rules of the convent, perpetuated disorder, and where reform of the monasteries appeared more necessary than ever. Above all, Hellenism was receding everywhere, and patriotism was at its last gasp.

Abroad, the peril was even greater. In the Balkan Peninsula, the Slavs shook off the yoke of the Empire. In Serbia, Stephen Nemanya extended his authority over Herzegovina, Montenegro, and Danubian Serbia, and founded a great state. Under the leadership of Peter and John Asen, the Bulgarians and the Wallachians revolted (1185), and, with the support of the Coumans and the concurrence of Stephen Nemanya, they made rapid progress. Isaac was defeated at Berrhœa (1190), and again at Arcadiopolis (1194). A Wallachian-Bulgarian empire was founded, whose Tsar, Johannitza, or Kalo-John (1197–1207), was to ensure its importance. By the treaty of 1201, Alexius III was compelled to confirm all the Bulgarian conquests, from Belgrade to the Black Sea and the Vardar. Soon afterward, the Bulgarian sovereign obtained from Innocent III the title of King, and the establishment of a national church (1204). This connoted the utter ruin of the work of Tzimisces and Basil II.

In the West, the horizon was still darker. The massacre of which the Latins in Constantinople had been the victims in 1182, at the time of the uprising that placed Andronicus Comnenus on the throne, had led to war with the Normans. True, the seizure of Thessalonica by the army of the King of Sicily had been a victory without results, and Isaac had succeeded in repelling the invaders (1186). But the old hostility between Westerners and Byzantines had been embittered by these events. The tactless policy of the Empire with regard to Frederic Barbarossa, at the time of the third Crusade (1189), had a similar effect. For a moment the German Emperor contemplated taking Constantinople, in concert with the Serbs and Bulgarians, and the Crusaders marched through the Empire like infuriated enemies. Henry VI, Barbarossa's son, was a still more dangerous foe, especially when he had inherited the domains and ambitions of the Norman kings. He dreamed of a conquest of the East; he called upon Alexius to restore to him all the territories formerly conquered by the Normans (1196), and compelled him, pending such restoration, to pay tribute.

But Venice especially was a disturbing factor. She, too, demanded vengeance for the massacres of 1182; and to appease her, Isaac was forced, in 1187, to grant

her ample indemnities and extensive privileges. In
1198, Alexius III was obliged to increase these concessions, whose effect he had, however, diminished by
conceding like reparations to the Genoese and the
Pisans. Notwithstanding this, the Venetians felt that
their commerce and their security were threatened by
the bitter hatred of the Greeks; and furthermore,
when Henry Dandolo was Doge (1193), they con-
ceived the idea that the conquest of the Byzantine
Empire would be the best solution of the difficulty
—the surest way to satisfy the accumulated Latin
grudges, and to make secure the interests of the Republic in the East.

From all these things—the hostility of the Papacy,
the ambition of Venice, the animosity of the whole
Latin world—was destined to emerge, as a necessary
consequence, the diversion of the fourth Crusade;
and before this formidable attack of the men of the
West, Byzantium, exhausted and enfeebled in the
East by the growth of the Slavic states, was incap-
able of resistance.

The Fourth Crusade.—In 1195, Alexius III, after
dethroning and blinding his brother Isaac, had im-
prisoned with the fallen sovereign his son, the young
Alexius. In 1201, the young prince escaped, and went
into the West, to seek assistance against the usurper.
It was just at the time when the army of the fourth
Crusade had assembled at Venice. The Venetians
seized eagerly the pretext thus afforded to interfere in
Byzantine affairs; and the magnificent promises that
Alexius made them readily overcame the scruples of

the Crusaders. Thus the shrewd policy of the Doge Dandolo diverted to Constantinople the expedition prepared for the deliverance of the Holy Land.

Early in 1203 the final compact was signed with the Byzantine pretender; on June 27, 1203, the Latin fleet anchored before Constantinople. The city was taken by assault on July 18, 1203, and Isaac Angelus was reseated on his throne, with his son, Alexius IV.

But the accord between the Greeks and the Westerners was of short duration. The new emperors were powerless to keep their promises; the Crusaders, especially the Venetians, made ever-increasing demands. On January 25, 1204, a national revolution overthrew the protégés of the West, and Alexius (V) Myrzuphlus, seized the power. Any sort of compromise became impossible. The Latins resolved to destroy the Byzantine Empire. On April 12, 1204, Constantinople was taken by assault, and pillaged without mercy. And while what was left of the aristocracy and clergy of Byzantium took refuge in Nicæa, to attempt to reconstitute the Empire there, the victors, in accordance with the treaty of partition signed in March, 1204, divided their conquest among them. A Latin emperor, Baldwin of Flanders, took his seat on the throne of the Comneni (May, 1204); a Latin king, Boniface of Montferrat, reigned at Thessalonica; a Venetian patriarch took possession of the patriarchal throne; over the entire territory of the vanquished Empire a crop of feudal lordships sprang into being. Above all, the Venetians, like the clever folk they were, made sure of all the places throughout the Orient that were important for the development of their commerce, and the foundation of their colonial empire.

It seemed that this was the end of Byzantium; and, in truth, the events of 1204 proved to be the blow from which the Byzantine Empire never recovered.

CHAPTER VII

The Latin Empire of Constantinople and the Greek Empire of Nicæa, 1204-1261

I. THE DISMEMBERMENT OF THE BYZANTINE EMPIRE

THE capture of Constantinople by the Crusaders resulted, first of all, in a profound alteration in the aspect of the Oriental world.

A crop of Latin feudal lordships sprang up on the ruins of the Byzantine Empire. A Latin empire was set up at Constantinople, and Baldwin, Count of Flanders, was chosen by the barons of the Crusade to be its sovereign; a kingdom of Thessalonica, theoretically a vassal of the Emperor, was created for the benefit of Marquis Boniface of Montferrat. There were titular dukes of Nicæa and Philippopolis, and lords of Demotika and Adramyttion. A few weeks later, the victorious march of Boniface of Montferrat as far as Athens and Corinth resulted in the founding of other Latin states—the Marquisate of Bodonitza, the Lordship of Negropont, the Duchy of Athens (ruled by the Burgundian family of La Roche), the Principality of Achaia or the Morea, which was conquered by Geoffrey of Villehardouin and William of Champlitte, Champagnards both, and which was destined to be the most permanent result in the Latin Orient of the Crusade of 1204.

On the other hand, Venice actually occupied Durazzo, on the coast of Epirus, Modon and Coron in the Peloponnesus, Crete and Eubœa, Gallipoli, Rodosto, Heraclea, and a considerable part of Constantinople, and instructed her patricians to settle on the islands of the Archipelago, where the Duchy of Naxos and the Marquisate of Cerigo, the Grand Duchy of Lemnos and the Lordship of Santorin were founded. And, as mistress of this splendid colonial empire, the Republic could legitimately permit her Doge to call himself "ruler of a quarter and a half of the Greek Empire."

The downfall of the Byzantine Empire gave birth in like manner to a multitude of Greek states. At Trebizond two princes, Alexius and David, descended from the Comneni, founded an empire which soon comprised the whole littoral of the Black Sea, from Heraclea to the Caucasus, and which was destined to endure until the middle of the fifteenth century (1461). In Epirus a bastard of the Angelus family, Michælangelo Comnenus, set up a despotat, which extended from Naupactus [Lepanto] to Durazzo. At Nicæa, Theodore Lascaris, son-in-law of Alexius (III) Angelus, gathered around him all that was left of the Byzantine aristocracy and higher clergy, and in 1206 he had himself solemnly crowned "Emperor of the Romans."

Other ambitious men, Gabalas at Rhodes, Mancaphas at Philadelphia, and Leo Sguros at Argos and Corinth, carved out for themselves other lordships from the rags and tatters of the Empire. It seemed that this was the end.

But, between these two new organisms thus ushered into political existence.there was a fundamental difference. The Latin Empire, notwithstanding the sterling qualities of its first two sovereigns, was destined to endure for hardly half a century (1204–1261); its initial weakness made it inevitably ephemeral. In the Greeks, on the contrary, the victory of the foreigner had reawakened patriotism, and revived the sentiment of Byzantine nationality. All these leaders, around whom were grouped all the living forces of the Greek world, had one and the same ambition—to recover Constantinople from the hated Latins. It only remained to be seen which of the two rival Greek empires, that of Nicæa or that of Epirus, would succeed in realizing this ambition.

II. THE LATIN EMPIRE OF CONSTANTINOPLE

THAT the work of the fourth Crusade should have any chance of permanence, it was necessary that the Empire should have a strong government, a closely centralized organization. Now, in the purely feudal state which the Latins had founded, the emperor was only the first of the barons. His authority, narrowly restricted territorially, was almost *nil* politically. Baldwin, immediately after his accession, was forced to declare war against his rebellious vassal, the King of Thessalonica; and although a successful effort was made to reconcile them, there was never a durable understanding between them.

Henry of Flanders, the successor of Baldwin, had to contend with the same difficulties; although, by dint of well-directed vigor, he succeeded in imposing his authority on Thessalonica (1209), and was recognized as suzerain by the feudatories of Greece at the parliament of Ravennika (1210), yet the latter, dukes of Athens and princes of Achaia, soon lost interest in the affairs of the Empire, and became almost independent.

The Latin Empire could expect but little from the Venetians, who were very jealous of their prerogatives, and selfishly absorbed by their own concerns. With the conquered Greeks no compact was possible. Despite the efforts made by several Latin sovereigns —Montferrat in Thessalonica and the Villehardouins in Achaia—to appease animosities and induce forgetfulness of the brutality of the conquest, the Greek people in general remained hostile to the foreigner, and awaited patiently a liberator, whether he should come from Epirus or from Nicæa.

Finally, to the inevitable Greek peril was added the possible Bulgarian peril. The Latins ill-advisedly rejected the alliance that Tsar Johannitza (1197–1207) proposed to them; and thus, instead of the assistance they might have received from the Bulgarians against the Byzantines, they made irreconcilable enemies of the former, who took part with the Greek sovereigns of Nicæa against the Latin Empire, and bent all their energies to its destruction.

Nevertheless, in the first moment of confusion that followed the capture of Constantinople, the Latins seemed likely to triumph everywhere. Thessaly, Central Greece, and the Peloponnesus were conquered in a few weeks, without serious resistance. In Asia Minor, Henry of Flanders defeated the Greeks at Poimamenum, and the newly born power of Theodore Lascaris, who retained little except Brousa, seemed on the verge of extinction, when the invasion of Thrace by the Bulgarians rescued it. Tsar Johannitza, in fact, attacked the whole Latin Empire, being well received everywhere by the insurgent Greek subjects. Rashly, with only a few troops, the Emperor Baldwin and the Doge Dandolo hastened to meet the enemy; the Latin army sustained a bloody defeat on the plains of Adrianople (1205), in which Baldwin disappeared. Then, for two years, the Bulgarian sovereign led his devastating armies through Macedonia, eager to avenge the defeats that Basil II had formerly inflicted upon his people, and proclaiming himself "Romaioctonus" (slayer of the Romans), by way of retort to "Bulgaroctonus." He was besieging Thessalonica when, fortunately for the Latins, he died, undoubtedly assassinated (1207).

Theodore Lascaris took advantage of this diversion to reëstablish and strengthen his own power. Nevertheless, under the government of Henry of Flanders, brother and successor of Baldwin (1205–1216),—who was assuredly the greatest ruler that the Latin Empire of Constantinople ever had,—it seemed probable that the state created by the Crusade would ensure its own permanence. After the death of Johannitza, Henry concluded a treaty with Bulgaria, thus delivering the Empire from a source of serious anxiety; he succeeded fairly well in reuniting the Latins, and in restoring the imperial authority over his great vassals; he even succeeded in obtaining the submission and sympathy of his Greek subjects. At the same time, he resumed the offensive in Asia, relying upon the Comneni of Trebizond. The first expedition, in 1206, gave him a part of Bithynia; in 1212 he displayed still greater energy, defeated Lascaris at Luparcus, and compelled him to cede to him a part of Mysia and of Bithynia.

But Henry died too soon (1216) for the empire of which he seemed destined to be the founder. From that time, the Greeks, as well as the Bulgarians, had a free hand; under the weak princes who governed it, the state founded by the Crusaders sank lower and lower to its deplorable end.

III. THE GREEK EMPIRE OF NICÆA

THEODORE LASCARIS (1206–1222) had become, step by step, the sole master of Byzantine Asia. He had defeated the sovereigns of Trebizond, who were jealous of his good fortune, defeated the Seljuk Turks (1211), and retaken from them a great part of the coasts of Anatolia. After the death of the Emperor Henry, he gave the Latins no respite. When he died, in 1222, leaving the throne to his son-in-law, John Vatatzes (1222–1254), he had reunited under his rule all of western Asia Minor, except the small portion of Bithynia still occupied by the Latins, and had carried his frontier to the head waters of the Sangarius and the Meander. During his long reign, Vatatzes, a good general as well as an able administrator, was to consummate the work of Lascaris, and to bring to Greek Asia Minor a last brief hour of prosperity.

But one might ask whether the destiny and ambition of the Empire of Nicæa would not always be confined within the Asiatic provinces of the ancient monarchy. In Europe, indeed, the despot of Epirus, Theodore Ducas Angelus (1214–1230), who succeeded his brother Michael, had largely augmented, at the expense of both Latins and Bulgarians, the states that he had inherited. He had recovered Durazzo and Corfu from the Venetians, and had occupied Ochrida and Pelagonia; in 1222, he seized Thessalonica, where young Demetrius, son of Boniface of Montferrat, was reigning; and in this city retaken from the Latins, he was solemnly crowned emperor, amid the acclamation of the Greeks, who saw in him the restorer of Hellenism. After this, at the expense of the Bulgarians, he extended his sphere of authority to the neighborhood of Adrianople, Philippopolis, and Christopolis, and it seemed that he would ere long overthrow the Latin Empire. At Serres, in 1224, he defeated the army of the impotent sovereign, Robert of Courtenay (1221–1228), who ruled over the remnants of the Latin state of Constantinople.

But the progress of the Greek Empire in Europe was about to be abruptly checked. John Asen, an alert and intelligent prince, reigned in Bulgaria from 1218 to 1241. Like Johannitza before him, he had readily taken sides with the Latins against the Greeks; and, when the Emperor Robert died in 1228, he was wholly disposed to accept the regency of the Latin Empire during the minority of the young Baldwin II (1228–1261). But the bungling intransigence of the Latin clergy was responsible for the preference over the orthodox prince being given to a cavalier as brave as he was politically incompetent—John of Brienne (1229–1237); and thus vanished the last chance of salvation for the Latin Empire. The Bulgarian sovereign, justly offended, became an irreconcilable enemy of the Latins, to the greater advantage of the Greeks of Nicæa. To these latter he rendered, at first, still further service, by laying low their rival in Europe, the Greek Emperor of Thessalonica, whose ambition was becoming disquieting to Bulgaria. Beaten and taken prisoner at Klokotnika (1230), Theodore was forced to abdicate, and the state he had founded, reduced to more modest proportions,—thereafter it comprised only Thessaly in addition to Thessalonica,—passed to his brother Manuel. Asen reinforced the power of Vatatzes by offering him an alliance (1234), at the same time that he thus rid him of his western rival. This meant the inevitable ruin of the Latin Empire.

The Emperor of Nicæa during the twelve years of his reign, had greatly enlarged his dominions. Conqueror of the Latins at Poimamenum (1224), he had taken the last strongholds that they possessed in Anatolia, had wrested from them the large islands of the Asiatic littoral,—Samos, Chios, Lesbos, and Cos,—and had compelled the Greek sovereign of Rhodes to become his vassal. He had sent an army into Thrace, and for a short time had occupied Adrianople, where he had attacked the Greek Emperor of Thessalonica. Finally, he attacked the Venetians in Crete. The Bulgarian alliance increased his power even more.

In 1236, the two allies united in a vigorous attack upon Constantinople. The city was near capitulation; but the West realized in time that she must be rescued: the maritime cities of Italy and the Prince of Achaia hastened to her aid. The capital of the Latin Empire escaped; and thanks to the rupture of the Greco-Bulgarian alliance, which followed closely upon the death of John Asen (1234) the hapless Latin monarchy endured for a quarter of a century longer—twenty-five years during which Baldwin II was forced to implore succor on all sides, without securing it; and, to obtain funds, was reduced to pawning the most precious relics in Constantinople, which Saint Louis bought from him; and he even reached such a pitch of destitution that he had to use the lead from the roofs with which to coin money, and in winter, to chop up the timbers of the imperial palaces, in order to keep warm

Meanwhile, Vatatzes succeeded in restoring Byzantine unity against the foreigner. He drove the Latins from their last possessions in Anatolia; he secured the powerful support of the Emperor Freceric II of Hohenstauffen, whose daughter he married (in 1244), and who, assuming the rôle of protector of the Latin Empire because he hated the Pope, unhesitatingly abandoned Constantinople to the Greeks; he deprived the Franks of the support of the Seljuk Sultan of Iconium (1244), and took advantage of the Mongol invasion in Asia Minor to enrich himself at the expense of the Turks.

He was especially active in Europe. The despotat of Epirus was a hotbed of anarchy; Vatatzes profited by this to compel John Angelus, son of Theodore, to renounce the title of emperor, and to acknowledge himself a vassal of Nicæa (1242). Four years later, in

1246, he seized Thessalonica, from which he ejected the despot Demetrius. He wrested from the Bulgarians a large part of Macedonia, Serres, Melnik, and Stenimachos; from the Latins, he took Bizye and Tzurulus (1247). Finally, he imposed his suzerainty, by force of arms, upon the only Greek prince who was still independent—the despot of Epirus, Michael II (1254). When Vatatzes died, on returning from this last campaign, the Greek Empire of Nicæa, rich, powerful, and prosperous, encircled on all sides the pitiful remnants of the Latin Empire. Constantinople alone remained to be conquered.

IV. THE RECAPTURE OF CONSTANTINOPLE BY THE GREEKS

THEODORE LASCARIS II (1254–1258), during his short reign, followed his father's policy. In 1255, at the pass of Rupel, he defeated the Bulgarians, who were endeavoring to take their revenge for the reverses inflicted upon them by Vatatzes, and forced peace upon them (1256); and, although he died too soon to put down the revolt of the scheming and ambitious despot of Epirus, Michael II, yet his successor, Michael Palæologus (1259–1261), won forgiveness, by his victories, for his usurpation and for the very unsavory way in which he thrust the legitimate dynasty from the throne. Michael of Epirus had made an alliance with Manfred, King of Sicily, and William of Villehardouin, Prince of Achaia; supported by the Albanians and Serbs, he was already threatening Thessalonica. Palæologus took the offensive, reconquered

Macedonia, invaded Albania, and inflicted a sanguinary defeat upon the despot and his allies, on the plain of Pelagonia (1259). Thus the despotat of Epirus vanished before the good fortune of the Empire of Nicæa. Shortly afterward Palæologus consummated his achievement by reconquering Constantinople.

In 1261, he crossed the Hellespont, and took from the Latins all that they possessed outside of the capital. With great adroitness, he entered into an alliance against the Venetians, who realized a little tardily the necessity of defending Constantinople, with their rivals, the Genoese, to whom, by the treaty of Nymphæum (1261), he pledged himself to grant all the privileges enjoyed by their competitors in the East. Therefore it needed only a propitious opportunity to deliver the capital into the hands of the Greeks. July 25, 1261, one of Palæologus's generals took advantage of the fact that the Venetian fleet had temporarily left the Golden Horn, to gain possession of the city by a lucky *coup de main*. Baıdwin II had no choice but to flee, followed by the Latin Patriarch and the Venetian colonists; and, on August 15, 1261, Michael Palæologus made his formal entry into Constantinople, and assumed the imperial crown in St. Sophia. The Byzantine Empire seemed to be born again, under the national dynasty of the Palæologi, who were to govern the realm for nearly two centuries.

V. THE PRINCIPALITY OF ACHAIA

THE other Latin states that grew out of the fourth Crusade did not all disappear at the same time with the Empire of Constantinople. To say nothing of Venice,—who was destined to retain for a long while to come her colonial empire in eastern waters, and the island lordships which her patricians had founded,— the Duchy of Athens, under the government of the La Roches, lasted until 1311; and, although as a result of the disastrous battle of Cephisus, it passed beneath the sway of the Catalans (1311–1333), whom the Florentine dukes of the Acciajuoli family (1333–1456) succeeded, the Byzantines never recovered possession of it.

The principality of Achaia, under the government of the three Villehardouins,—Geoffrey I, founder of the dynasty, and his sons Geoffrey II and William (1209–1278),—was even more flourishing. Despite its purely feudal constitution, and the twelve great baronies which the Frankish conquest set up there, the country, skilfully administered by its sovereigns, was one of the most prosperous states in the Latin Orient during the whole thirteenth century. The finances were in excellent condition; the army was supposed to be composed of "the best chivalry in Europe"; its tranquillity was undisturbed, and its cordial relations with its Greek subjects were remarkable. The court of Andravida was, says a chronicler, "more brilliant than that of the greatest kings." French influence was all-powerful; "the people there spoke French as well as they did in Paris."

In the curious book called the *Chronicle of Morea*, we see this society, reminiscent of France and of the days of chivalry, live again as it were; just as to-day, throughout the Peloponnesus, at Acrocorinth or

Klemutsi, at Karytaina or Mistra, at Kalamata or Maina, we find the ruins of the strong feudal fortresses built by the French masters of the country. And it is assuredly not one of the least interesting episodes in Byzantine history—this power of seduction which the far-distant France of the thirteenth century exerted in this Greek country, conquered by force of arms, and so quickly assimilated.

But the disaster of Pelagonia, where William of Villehardouin fell into the hands of Michael Palæologus, had momentous consequences for the principality of Achaia. In order to recover his liberty, the French prince was compelled, by the treaty of 1262, to cede Monemvasia, Maina, and Mistra to the Greeks. Thus the Byzantines regained a foothold in the Peloponnesus. During the governments of women and foreigners—Angevin princes and the Navarrese crowd—which followed the death of Villehardouin (1278), the Byzantines were destined, with the support of the indigenous population, to make rapid progress in that region, and to found there, in the fourteenth century, the Despotat of Morea, which was to be one of the most interesting states in the decadence of Byzantium.

Notwithstanding this, the fact remains that the fourth Crusade left the Orient filled with Latin settlements. Despite the recovery of Constantinople, despite the victories won by Michael Palæologus in Epirus and Achaia, this fact was destined to be a source of constant anxiety and of undeniable weakness to the restored empire of the Palæologi.

CHAPTER VIII

The Byzantine Empire under the Palæologi
1261-1453

I. THE POSITION OF THE GREEK EMPIRE IN 1261

THE Empire, as it was reconstituted under the new dynasty of the Palæologi, bore but little resemblance to the realm over which the Comneni had reigned. In Asia, the Empire of Trebizond possessed the majority of the provinces bordering on the Black Sea, and formed an independent state which drew further and further away from Byzantium, and, down to the middle of the fifteenth century, led an existence parallel to that of the Greek Empire. In Europe, the despotat of Epirus occupied the southern part of Albania and a part of Ætolia; the Duchy of Neopatras, or Great Wallachia, comprised Thessaly, Locris, and Phthiotis. Beside these Greek states, there was a Latin Duchy of Athens in central Greece, and in the Peloponnesus a Latin Principality of Morea. The Venetians were masters of most of the islands in the Archipelago; the Genoese held Chios, and had important colonies on the coast of Anatolia and on the Black Sea.

The reconstructed Greek Empire comprised only

three groups of demesnes in Asia, the possessions of the former Empire of Nicæa; in Europe, Constantinople, with Thrace, and a part of Macedonia, of which Thessalonica was the principal city; and, lastly, several islands, as Rhodes, Lesbos, Samothrace, and Imbros. And confronting this Empire, shorn of territory, financially exhausted, and feeble militarily, were young states, vigorous, conscious of their power, keen to contend with Byzantium for the hegemony she had once possessed. These states were — in the Balkan Peninsula, the second Bulgarian Empire in the thirteenth century, and the Greater Serbia of Stephen Dushan in the fourteenth; and, most important of all, in Asia, the Turks, whose attitude became more menacing and formidable day by day. It was a far cry back to the time when Constantinople was the centre of the Oriental world and of civilization.

The Reign of Michael (VIII) Palæologus (1261–1282).—To restore the Byzantine Empire in its integrity, and in all its old-time splendor, would have required a prodigious effort. Michael VIII (1261–1282) attempted it; and, although he did not succeed in realizing to the full his far-reaching ambition, he seems, none the less, in respect of the goal that he set before himself, of his genius for administration, and his adroitness, to have been the last of the great emperors of Byzantium.

Immediately after his accession, Michael made plain his purpose to recover, from the Greeks as well as the Latins, the provinces wrested from the Empire. He obtained a foothold in Frankish Morea (end of

1261); he took Janina from the Epirots (1265); a part of Macedonia from the Bulgarians (1264); and several islands in the Archipelago from the Venetians; he put down the insolence of the Genoese; he placed the Serbian and Bulgarian churches once more under the authority of a Greek prelate (1272).

But he very soon encountered the hostility of the West. The Papacy and Venice had never abandoned the idea of restoring the Latin Empire; the new sovereign of the Two Sicilies, Charles of Anjou, by virtue of the treaty of Viterbo (1267) inheritor of the claims of Baldwin II, and suzerain of the Principality of Achaia by the marriage of his son with the heiress of Villehardouin, cherished far more ambitious designs with respect to the Orient. He conquered Corfu (1267), occupied Durazzo and the coast of Epirus (1272), assumed the title of King of Albania, and allied himself with all the enemies of the Empire—Bulgarians, Serbs, and the Prince of Greater Wallachia.

At this formidable crisis the supreme diplomatic skill of Michael Palæologus prevented a general coalition of the West against the Byzantines. Taking advantage of the inquietude of the Papacy, which was not anxious to see the power of Charles of Anjou grow beyond measure, encouraging the longing that the sovereign pontiffs always felt to restore the authority of Rome over the Greek Church, he concluded with Gregory X, at the Council of Lyons (1274), the pact which subordinated the Eastern Church anew to the Papacy.

But, in exchange, Michael VIII received the assurance that there should be no further contest as to his possession of Constantinople; that he should have a free hand in the East, and that he should be permitted to combat the Latins themselves there. And, in fact, he did take the offensive in Epirus (1274) against the Angevin troops; he intervened in Thessaly, where he besieged Neopatras (1275); fought the Venetians in Eubœa, and pushed forward into Achaia, where the death of William of Villehardouin (1278) greatly weakened the Frankish principality.

Unfortunately, the insuperable hostility of the Greeks to Rome interfered with these adroit combinations. Michael VIII had imposed the union upon the Byzantine clergy by force; he proposed, in concert with the Patriarch John Beccus (1275), to carry it out by force. Thereby he succeeded only in stirring up a schism within the Orthodox Church; and the antagonism between the two realms, which he had believed that he could abate, became only the more bitter and more to be feared.

On his part, Charles of Anjou, who was badly disgruntled, did not disarm. He reorganized his government in Epirus (1278), won the Papacy over to his views (1281), and formed with Rome and Venice a league to restore the Latin Empire, which league, from hatred for Michael VIII, the Serbs joined and the Bulgarians, and even the Greeks of Thessaly and Epirus. The Byzantine Emperor made head against them all. At Berat he defeated the generals of Charles of Anjou; above all, to shatter the ambition of the Angevin, he instigated the Sicilian Vespers (March, 1282). But although by this means he finally held the West in check, Michael VIII, being too exclusively absorbed by his schemes with regard to the Latins, was culpably oblivious of the Turkish peril, which was looming up in Asia Minor, and of the growing Serbian peril in Europe. Another source of weakness to the monarchy was the religious agitation that he had incited within the Empire. The reign of Michael VIII had seemed to mark the beginning of a renaissance of the Empire; decadence, swift and unavoidable, was soon to follow.

II. THE GREEK EMPIRE UNDER THE LAST OF THE PALÆOLOGI (1282–1453)

THE decadent tendency speedily became manifest under the successors of Michael VIII—his son Andronicus II (1282–1328), an educated prince, a fine orator, friend of men of letters, and very pious, but incurably weak and commonplace; and the latter's grandson Andronicus III (1328–1341), intelligent, but frivolous, turbulent, and a high liver; it was manifest during the long reign of John V (1341–1391), despite the energetic impetus momentarily given to affairs by that remarkable ruler, the usurper John (VI) Cantacuzene (1341–1355), and despite the notable qualities brought to the throne later by Manuel II (1391–1425), son of John V, a prince of eminent ability, of whom it had been well said that "in better times he would have saved the Empire if the Empire could have been saved."

The Empire could not be saved. John VIII[1] (1425–1448) and Constantine XIII (1448–1453) were able

1 John V and John VIII are more usually called John Palæologus I and II.—*Trans.*

neither to arrest its degeneration nor to prevent its destruction; and the latter could do no more than seek death heroically on the ramparts of his capital when it was taken by storm. It mattered little, therefore, that during this century and a half the Empire sometimes had at its head men of worth: events were stronger than their wills; both within and without, the causes of dissolution were without remedy.

Internal Causes of Decadence. The Civil War—To make head against the perils which menaced the Empire from abroad, it was essential that it should be united, peaceful, and strong at home. On the contrary, the epoch of the Palæologi was filled with revolutions and civil strife. The grandson of Andronicus II, the future Emperor Andronicus III, rose against his grandfather, who designed to deprive him of his legitimate claim to the throne; and for several years (1321–1328), the war, interrupted by occasional truces, devastated the Empire, to end finally in the capture of Constantinople by the insurgents, and the fall of Andronicus II.

During the regency of Anne of Savoy and the minority of John (V) Palæologus, John Cantacuzene, in his turn, proclaimed himself emperor (1341), and for six years (1341–1347) the Greek world was divided into two factions,—the aristocracy supporting the usurper and the people the legitimate dynasty,—until the day when the capital fell, through treachery, into the hands of the pretender.

During the reign of John Cantacuzene (1347–1355), the intrigues of John (V) Palæologus, for whom the new Emperor had set aside his share of the imperial authority, kept the Empire constantly in commotion, and instigated a fresh revolution, which overthrew Cantacuzene. Then there were the broils of John V with his son Andronicus IV (1376), and with his grandson John VII (1391), both of whom succeeded in removing the old sovereign temporarily from the throne. And the most serious thing was that, in the course of these dissensions, the adversaries did not scruple to call to their aid all the enemies of the Empire,—Bulgarians, Serbs, Turks,—paying them for their assistance with extensive subsidies, even with cessions of territory, and thus opening the door to those who contemplated the destruction of the monarchy. All patriotism, even all political insight, had disappeared in the conflict between those frenzied ambitions.

The Social and Religious Disputes.—Religious and social antagonisms aggravated the desolation of the civil commotions. Toward the middle of the fourteenth century, a wave of social revolution passed over the Empire: the lower classes revolted against the aristocracy of birth and of wealth; and for seven years (1342 to 1349), Thessalonica, the second city of the Empire, through the agitation of the Zealots was alive with disturbances, terror, and bloodshed. The Macedonian city constituted itself a veritable independent republic, whose tumultuous history is one of the most absorbing episodes in the life of the Greek Empire during the fourteenth century; and it was not without great difficulty that John Cantacuzene finally restored order and tranquillity in the city that had taken sides against him.

Religious conflicts, due especially to the immemorial hostility between Greeks and Latins, intensified the confusion. Michael VIII deemed it wise, as a matter of policy, to draw nearer to Rome and to renew the union between the churches; by so doing, he aroused a disaffection so serious, that the first care of his successor, Andronicus II, was to make his peace with the Orthodox clergy, by denouncing the pact concluded with the Papacy. This naturally embittered the antagonism between Latins and Greeks, and, in the monarchy itself, the dissension between the partisans and adversaries of the union. A hot polemical controversy fostered this agitation, and imperceptibly transformed all sympathy with Latin ideas into downright treachery to the country.

Under these conditions, the slightest pretext unleashed the hatred of Byzantine nationalism for the West. This was the underlying cause of the controversy, outwardly purely theological, called the quarrel of the Hesychasts, which agitated and divided the Empire for ten years (1341–1351). In this affair, apparently the fruit of the strange visions of a few monks at Mount Athos, the adversaries were, in reality, the Greek mind and the Latin mind—Oriental mysticism, represented by the Hesychasts and their champion, Gregory Palamas, and Latin rationalism, whose champions were a Barlaam and an Akindynos, fed on St. Thomas Aquinas, and trained in the dialectics of the scholiasts; and it was for this reason that the quarrel soon took on a political color, Cantacuzene taking sides with Mount Athos, and Anne of Savoy with Barlaam.

The same thing happened when, from political necessity, John V (1369), and, later, Manuel II (1417) reopened negotiations with Rome; and John VIII, to avert the Turkish peril, tried a desperate expedient. The Emperor went in person to Italy (1437), and at the Council of Florence, signed with Pope Eugene IV the agreement that put an end to the schism. Like Michael VIII, he came in collision with the savage bigotry of the Orthodox clergy and people, who were persuaded that, in the face of all their promises, the Latins aimed at nothing less than "the destruction of the Greek city and race and name." John VIII and his successor, Constantine XIII, attempted in vain to impose union by force: insurrection rumbled under the arches of St. Sophia (1452); on the eve of the catastrophe which was to engulf Constantinople, the people of the city took sides hotly for or against the union, and some men declared that they "would prefer to see the Turkish turban reign in Byzantium rather than the Latin mitre."

Financial and Military Disorder.—In addition to all the rest, there was the confusion in the finances. Despite the fiscal tyranny, the land-tax, in a country completely ruined by war, brought only insufficient resources into the treasury. Customs duties diminished with increasing rapidity after the commerce of the Empire fell into the hands of Venetians and Genoese. The government was reduced to debasing the coinage, and the Emperor to borrowing, and pawning the crown jewels; money there was none: the treasury was empty.

The military deterioration was no less serious: the army, numerically weak, ill-disciplined, and with difficulty kept in hand, became gradually more and more powerless to defend the Empire. The mercenaries in the service of the government revolted against it, as did, under Andronicus II, the Catalan Grand Company, which, having seized Gallipoli, besieged Constantinople for two years (1305–1307), and carried its victorious standards across Macedonia and Greece (1307–1311); as did, in the middle of the fourteenth century, the Serbian and Turkish auxiliaries, who ravaged and sacked the Empire without mercy.

At sea there was the same helplessness. Michael VIII had endeavored to reorganize the Byzantine fleet; his successors decided that the expense was useless, and abandoned the control of the eastern waters to the fleets of the Italian republics. The Empire was falling into decay, powerless against the perils that threatened it from without.

External Causes of Decadence. Bulgarians and Serbs. After John Asen's death in 1241, the Wallachian-Bulgarian Empire, which had been so great a menace to Byzantium since the end of the twelfth century, had been seriously weakened by the intestine wars that tore it asunder. The severe defeat that the Serbs inflicted upon the Tsar Michael at Velbujd (1330) definitively destroyed its power. Nevertheless, the Bulgarians were still unpleasant neighbors to the Empire: they interfered in Byzantine affairs; they took advan-

tage of the assistance they gave to Andronicus II and
Anne of Savoy to demand extensive cessions of territory; Greece, above all, was terribly ravaged by their
constant raids.

But the Serbs had come to be the most redoubtable
foes of Byzantium. Under the successors of Stephen
Nemanya,—Urosh I (1243–1276), Dragutin (1276–
1282), and Milutin (1282–1321),—Serbia had grown,
at the expense of the Bulgarians and the Greeks, until
she had become the most important state in the
Balkan Peninsula. Urosh I had conquered the upper
valley of the Vardar (1272); Milutin, relying upon the
alliance of the Epirots and Angevins, had occupied
Uskub (1282), and conquered the district of Serres
and Christopolis, which gave him access to the Archipelago (1283); had laid hands upon Ochrida, Prespa,
and all of Western Macedonia, invaded northern Albania (1296), and compelled Andronicus II to recognize all his conquests (1298); and, like the Bulgarians,
the Serbs had interfered continually in the internal
disturbances of the Greek Empire.

When Stephen Dushan (1331–1355) ascended the
throne, Serbia extended from the Save and the Danube in the north to Strumitza and Prilip in the south,
from Bosna in the west to Rilodagh and the Stroma in
the east. Dushan resolved to make her even greater:
he dreamed of uniting the whole Balkan Peninsula
under his rule, and of assuming the imperial crown at
Constantinople. A shrewd diplomat and a great general, intelligent, strong-willed, and tenacious, he began
by completing the conquest of Western Macedonia
(1334); next wresting Albania as far as Durazzo and

Valona from the Angevins, and Epirus as far as Janina from the Greeks (1340), he forced his way into Macedonia, where the Byzantines still held only Thessalonica and Chalcidice, and where the Serbian frontier touched the Maritza on the east (1345). And in 1346, in the cathedral of Uskub, Dushan had himself solemnly crowned "Emperor and Autocrat of the Serbians and Romans."

The Serbian Empire now reached from the Danube to the Ægean Sea and the Adriatic. Dushan organized it on the model of Byzantium. He gave it a code of laws (1349); he established a patriarchate at Ipek, independent of Constantinople; having overcome the Greeks (he besieged Thessalonica in 1351), the Angevins, the King of Bosnia, and the King of Hungary, he stood forth as the most powerful prince in the Balkans, and the Pope proclaimed him "leader of the war against the Turks." It remained for Dushan only to take Constantinople. He tried it (1355), took Adrianople and Thrace, and died suddenly,—unfortunately for Christendom,—in sight of the city which he had dreamed of making his capital. After his death his Empire speedily fell apart. But from this struggle of twenty-five years Byzantium emerged a little weaker than before.

The Turks.—While the Greek Empire in Europe was thus dwindling before the attacks of the Slavic states, the Osmanli Turks were making progress in Asia, under the leadership of the three great chiefs, Ertoghrul, Osman (1289–1326), and Orkhan (1326–1359). Despite the efforts, sometimes successful, of

Andronicus II to arrest their progress, Brusa fell into the hands of the Ottomans (1326), who established their capital there. Nicæa succumbed next (1329), then Nicomedia (1337); in 1338 the Turks reached the Bosphorus. They soon crossed the strait, at the invitation of the Byzantines themselves, who eagerly sought their assistance in their civil conflicts. In 1353, Cantacuzene, who in 1346 had given his daughter in marriage to the Sultan, rewarded his services by ceding to him a fortress on the European side of the Dardanelles. In the following year (1354), the Turks established themselves at Gallipoli; they occupied Demotica and Tzurulus in 1357. The Balkan Peninsula lay open before them.

Murad I (1359–1389) grasped the opportunity. In 1361 he conquered Thrace, which John V was compelled to recognize as his (1363); he captured Philippopolis, and, soon after, Adrianople, whither he transferred his capital (1365). Byzantium, isolated, surrounded, cut off from the rest of the monarchy, awaited, entrenched behind her walls, the supreme blow, which seemed inevitable.

Meanwhile, the Turks completed the conquest of the Balkan Peninsula. At the Maritza they crushed the southern Serbs and the Bulgarians (1371); they set up their colonies in Macedonia, and threatened Thessalonica (1374); they invaded Albania (1386), destroyed the Serbian Empire on the field of Kossovo (1389), and transformed Bulgaria into a Turkish pashalik (1393). John V was fain to do homage as a vassal of the Sultan, to pay him tribute, and to supply him with a contingent of troops to take the last stronghold that the Byzantines still possessed in Asia Minor — Philadelphia (1391).

Bajazet (1389–1402) took even more forcible measures in dealing with the Empire. He laid close siege to the Greek capital (1391–1395); and when the supreme attempt of the West to save Byzantium had failed, at the battle of Nicopolis (1396), he made a vigorous attack on Constantinople (1397), at the same time that he invaded the Morea. Fortunately for the Greeks, the Mongol invasion and the crushing defeat that Timur inflicted upon the Turks at Angora (1402) gave the Empire twenty years further respite. But in 1421 Murad II (1421–1451) resumed the offensive. He attacked—without success, it is true—Constantinople, which resisted vigorously (1422); he took Thessalonica (1430), which the Venetians had bought from the Greeks in 1423; one of his generals forced his way into the Morea (1423); he himself carried the war into Bosnia and Albania, and extorted tribute from the Prince of Wallachia. The Greek Empire, at its last gasp, had nothing left besides Constantinople and the vicinity, as far as Derkos and Selymbria, except a few scattered districts along the coast—Anchialus, Mesembria, Athos, and the Peloponnesus, which, having been almost entirely recovered from the Latins, became at this time the centre, as it were, of Greek nationality.

Despite the heroic efforts of John Hunyady, who defeated the Turks in 1443 at Kunoviza; despite the resistance of Scanderbeg in Albania, the Ottomans pursued their advantage. In 1444, at the battle of Varna, the last great effort that Christendom essayed in the East was foiled; the Duchy of Athens submitted to the Turks; the Principality of Morea, being invaded, was compelled to pay tribute (1446); John Hunyady was defeated at the second battle of Kossovo (1448). Constantinople alone survived, an impregnable citadel, and seemed to constitute, in herself alone, the whole Empire. But for her, too, the end was at hand. When Mohammed II ascended the throne (1451), he was firmly resolved to possess himself of the city.

Byzantium and the Latins.—Instead of aiding in the defence of the Empire, the Latins who were settled in the East, Venetians and Genoese, had done nothing except selfishly take advantage of her distress and hasten her destruction.

Established by Michael Palæologus at Galata, opposite Constantinople (1267), and settled on the coast of Asia Minor and on the Black Sea, the Genoese had, according to a Greek historian, "closed to the Romans all the routes of maritime commerce"; and although the Greeks, in the reign of Andronicus III, had for the moment retaken from them Chios (1329), Lesbos (1336), and Phocæa (1340), these ephemeral triumphs had diminished neither the insolence nor the greed for gain of the foreign merchants.

The Venetians, being masters of the Archipelago, with speedy access to Constantinople and Thessalonica, were no less to be feared. The two republics bore themselves in the Empire as in a conquered country, defying the Byzantine sovereigns, and imposing their will upon them by force; filling the capital with disorder and murders, forcing their fleets into the Golden Horn, inciting revolution in the capital (1375), compelling by threats the cession of territory or the granting of privileges; establishing—as the Genoese did in 1348—a naval station in the Bosphorus; robbing Greek subjects, and attacking Constantinople itself,—as the Venetian did in 1305, and the Genoese in 1348,—when they thought that they had ground for complaint against the emperor.

The Byzantines, although indignant, swallowed these insults, as they were powerless to repel them by force; and Venetians and Genoese took advantage of this state of affairs to exploit the monarchy. Venice set up a colonial empire in the waters of the Levant. Genoa organized, in reconquered Chios (1347), the powerful commercial association called the *Maona*. The Latins, according to a Byzantine historian, "had taken unto themselves all the wealth of the Byzantines, and nearly all the revenues from the sea," thus consummating the economic ruin of the Empire.

The rest of the West ceased to concern itself about Byzantium. It is true that the Crusade of 1343 had recovered Smyrna for a few years, and that of 1366 had momentarily taken Gallipoli from the Turks. It is true that Christendom had in 1396 put forth the mighty effort that ended in the disaster of Nicopolis, and in 1444 that which ended in the disaster of Varna; and, again, during the two years from 1397 to 1399, the French Marshal Boucicault had gallantly defended Constantinople against the assaults of the Turks. But the fact is that the West had become indifferent to the Byzantine 'Empire, or now turned its thoughts toward it only to take advantage of its wretched plight to dominate it religiously, to conquer it politically, and to exploit it economically. The Papacy thought only of reëstablishing the union of the churches, not disturbing itself about the repugnance with which the Byzantines regarded it. The princes of the West thought only of dividing up the Empire. To no purpose did John V in 1369, Manuel II in 1402, and John VIII in 1439, go to Italy, to France, to England, to beg for assistance: they obtained only a courteous reception and fine promises. And when Mohammed II resolved to make an end of the Greek Empire, Byzantium, worn out and abandoned, had nothing left to do but die.

The Capture of Constantinople by the Turks.—And that is what she did. On his accession, Manuel II had made his purposes manifest, by building on the Bosphorus the fortress of Roumeli-Hissar, which closed communication between Constantinople and the Black Sea, and, on the other hand, by sending an expedition into Morea (1452) to prevent the Greek despots of Mistra from succoring the capital. Before long, the Sultan attacked the city (April 5, 1483). Against the formidable Turkish army, which contained nearly 160,000 men, the Emperor Constantine XIII could oppose barely 9000 soldiers, half of whom, at least, were foreigners. The Greeks, because of their hostility to the religious union reëstablished by their sovereign, did their duty, in general, very badly. Nevertheless, despite the strength of the Turkish artillery and the formidable cannon of the engineer Urban, the first assault was repulsed (April 18). But

Mohammed II succeeded in bringing his fleet into the Golden Horn, and thus threatened another sector of the ramparts. The assault of May 7 failed, also; but a breach was made in the ramparts of the town, near the Gate of St. Romanus.

In the night of May 28–29, 1453, the supreme assault began. Twice the Turks were repulsed; then Mohammed hurled the Janissaries into the breach. At that moment, the Genoese Giustiniani, who, with the Emperor, had been the soul of the defence, was badly wounded, and was compelled to quit his post, thus disorganizing the defence. Nevertheless, the Emperor fought gallantly on, until a party of the enemy, forcing the postern called Xyloporta, assailed the defenders in the rear.

This was the end. Constantine XIII was slain in the breach, like a hero, thus shedding upon Byzantium one final ray of splendor. But the Turks were masters of the city. Then in fallen Constantinople there ensued pillage and massacre; more than 60,000 persons were taken into captivity. And on May 30, 1453, at eight in the morning, Mohammed II made his triumphal entry into Byzantium, and went to St. Sophia, to return thanks to the God of Islam.

III. BYZANTINE CIVILIZATION IN THE TIME OF THE PALÆOLOGI

So great was the vitality of this Byzantine civilization, even in its decadence, that a last renaissance, literary and artistic, illumined with a ray of expiring glory the epoch of the Palæologi.

THE PALÆOLOGI

In the world of the fourteenth and fifteenth centuries, Constantinople was still one of the most beautiful and renowned cities in the universe; the metropolis of the orthodox faith, whither the Greek and Slavic pilgrims of the Orient came in multitudes; the great mart of commerce, where the merchants of the whole West came together; the magnificent and fruitful center of a notable intellectual and artistic culture. The schools of the Byzantine capital were more flourishing and more frequented than ever; the illustrious professors of the University,—Planudes, Moschopulus, Triklinius, early in the fourteenth century; and, later, Chrysoloras and Argyropulus,—reviving the study of the classical authors, approved themselves the worthy precursors of the humanists of the Renaissance. By their side the philosophers, Gemistus Plethon and Bessarion kept alive the tradition of the study of the Platonic doctrines, and prepared to transmit them to the West. And there, too, was a whole pleiad of original and individual talents—historians like John Cantacuzene and Nicephorus Gregoras in the fourteenth century, Phrantzes, Ducas, Chalcondylas, and Critobulus in the fifteenth; theologians like Gregory Palamas and the two Cabasilas in the fourteenth century, Marcus Eugenicus and George Scholarius in the fifteenth; orators like Nicephorus Chumnos and Demetrius Cydones; essayists like Theodore Metochite and Manuel Palæologus; poets like Manuel Philes; satirists like the anonymous author of the *Descent of Mazaris into Hell*. The sciences—astronomy, medicine, and natural history—were cultivated as zealously as literature; and it can justly be said of the scholars of that time that they rendered no less important services than did a Roger Bacon in the West. It seems, in very truth, as if, on the eve of her downfall, Byzantium mustered all her intellectual powers, to give forth one final ray of light.

And in like manner, at the dawn of the fifteenth century, Byzantine art awoke to a last new birth. Reverting to its most ancient sources, particularly to that Alexandrine tradition of which the humanists of the time revived the influence, this art lost its abstract character, to become living and picturesque—sentimental, dramatic, and charming, in turn. Iconography took on a new and richer life, more sympathetic and more impassioned. Color, harmoniously and skilfully employed, was almost impressionistic in its technique.

Schools arose, diverse in their sources of inspiration and in their methods: the school of Constantinople whose *chef-d'œuvre* is the mosaics of Kahrie-Djami (early fourteenth century); the Macedonian school, whose masters decorated the churches of Macedonia, Old Serbia, and the oldest churches of Athos, and of which the famous Manuel Panselinos, in the sixteenth century, was, perhaps, the last representative; the Cretan school, of which the frescoes of Mistra are unquestionably the masterpiece.

Thus Byzantium, though in appearance exhausted, took on new vigor in the fourteenth century, as formerly in the tenth, at the touch of the ancient tradition; and by virtue of this potent advance in art, which may be compared to the Italian Renaissance of the fourteenth century, although in no way indebted to it, the influence of Byzantium was felt once more throughout the whole Near East, among the Serbs, the Russians, and the Roumanians.

The Despotat of Mistra.—Among these various centers of intellectual and artistic culture, Mistra deserves special mention. Founded by William of Villehardouin, above the plain where Sparta had been, and, later, the residence of the Greek despots of the Peloponnesus, Mistra, with its churches embellished with frescoes, with its walls, its houses, and palaces, was, as has been well said, the Byzantine Pompeii. After the city had fallen again under Byzantine domination, in 1262, Andronicus II devoted himself to peopling it and embellishing it, and he built several churches there. Later, John Cantacuzene gave even more attention to the city. Of the province of the Morea, reconquered bit by bit from the Franks, he made an appanage for his younger son Manuel who received the title of Despot (1348); and under the rule of this prince, as well as under that of the younger members of the Palæologus dynasty who succeeded him (beginning in 1383), Mistra was the center of a brilliant court, artistic and intellectual, a veritable focus of Hellenism and humanism, and a place of refuge for the expiring Greek nationality.

It is, indeed, a fact worthy of note that in this Byzantium, which had so long ago become indifferent to ancient Greece, there should suddenly come to life again, on the eve of the catastrophe, the memory of its distant Hellenic origin. The great names of Pericles and Themistocles, of Lycurgus and Epaminondas, came unexpectedly from the lips of the men of the fifteenth century, who delighted to recall what they did in the old days, "for the public welfare and for their country." The most noted men of the time, Gemistus Plethon and Bessarion, saw in the revival of the Hellenic tradition the leaven which would save the Empire, and they adjured the sovereigns to assume, instead of the outworn title of Basileus of the Romans, the new and living name of King of the Hellenes, "which, in itself," they said, "would suffice to ensure the salvation of the Hellenes, and the deliverance of their enslaved brethren." Bessarion reminded the last of the Palæologi of the exploits of the Spartans of old, and implored him to place himself at the head of their descendants, in order to free Europe from the Turks, and to reconquer in Asia the heritage of his fathers. On the eve of the supreme catastrophe, Plethon proposed to Manuel II a long programme of reforms for regenerated Hellas. And vain as these illusions may seem, at the moment when Mohammed II was at the very gates, it is none the less a remarkable thing, this reawakening of the consciousness of the Hellenism that refused to die; this prophetic vision of the distant future, when, in the words of Chalcondylas, a fifteenth-century author, "a Greek king and his successors shall one day restore a realm wherein the reunited sons of the Hellenes will administer their own affairs and build up a nation."

It was at the court of Mistra that these aspirations chiefly found expression; and, too, it is in the churches of Mistra—the Metropole (early fourteenth century), the Peribleptos (mid-fourteenth century), and the

Pantanassa (fifteenth century)—that we find some of the masterpieces of the artistic renaissance of that time. One detects there a rare understanding of decorative significance; a striving for the picturesque, for movement, for expression: a remarkable taste for refinement and grace; an admirable sense of color, at once delicate and vigorous; an art both intelligent and free. The same qualities are found in the frescoes of the Macedonian churches as in the most ancient paintings of the monasteries of Athos. They show how great was the creative originality of which Byzantine art was still capable, and reflect supreme splendor upon the epoch of the Palæologi.

The Greek Empire of Trebizond.—At the other extremity of the Byzantine realm, at the head of the Black Sea, the distant Empire of Trebizond presented, at about the same time, another interesting center of Hellenic civilization.

Early in the thirteenth century, undeterred by the attacks of the sovereigns of Nicæa, and of the Seljuk Turks, Alexius I, of the Comnenus family (1204–1222), had founded a state which comprised all of the ancient Polemaniacus Pontus, and extended as far east as the Phasis. But, isolated as it was at the farthest extremity of the Orient, lost between the Turks and the Mongols, convulsed within by the quarrels of its turbulent feudal nobility, exploited by the Genoese, coveted by the Greek sovereigns of Constantinople, the new Empire was often in difficulties.

Nevertheless, it knew prosperous days, under Alexius II (1297–1330), and under the long reign of Alexius

III, who embellished his capital with churches and monasteries. Terraced above the sea, among running streams and verdure, immensely rich by favor of her extensive commerce with the interior of Asia, celebrated for her magnificence and the beauty of her princesses, Trebizond was at that time one of the most beautiful cities in the Orient, and one of the great markets of the world. The palace of the princes, on a plateau overlooking the coast, was a marvel of refined magnificence; and the fame of the city, "the head and eye of all Asia," had spread far and wide throughout the East.

Undoubtedly, from the early years of the fifteenth century, the court of the Comneni was thoroughly demoralized; its history is replete with sanguinary intrigues and tragic episodes. None the less, thanks to the Empire of Trebizond, there still remained at the head of the Pontus Euxinus, a reflection of the glories of Byzantium; and for two and one half centuries Greek nationalism found a refuge there.

The Despotat of Morea and the Empire of Trebizond were to survive the fall of Constantinople only a few years. In 1453, the Albanian insurrection in the Peloponnesus had brought the Turks into Morea; and the despots, brothers of Constantine XIII, after summoning the Turks to their succor, were forced to acknowledge themselves vassals of the Sultan. When Thomas refused to pay tribute, in 1459, the situation became more serious. Mohammed II appeared in person in Morea, breaking down all resistance, but failed to gain possession of Mistra. Once more the despots had to submit, but soon they rebelled again. There-

upon the Sultan marched straight upon Mistra, and
deposed the Despot Demetrius, whom he carried off
a prisoner; the other Greek prince fled to Italy, and
Morea became a Turkish province (1460).

David Comnenus, the last Emperor of Trebizond,
succumbed in 1461. He had tried in vain to avail himself of the support of his niece's husband, the Turco-
man Prince Ouzoun Hassan. In 1461, Mohammed II
appeared in Anatolia, defeated Hassan's troops, then
turned against Trebizond, which had to capitulate.
The remaining members of the imperial family were
imprisoned, by order of the Sultan, near Serres in
Macedonia. This was the end of the last Greek state
in the Orient.

Thus perished the Byzantine Empire, after an existence of more than one thousand years, and an existence often glorious; after it had been for centuries the
champion of Christendom against Islam, the defender
of civilization against barbarism, the educator of the
Slavic East; after it had made its influence felt even
in the West. But, although Byzantium had fallen, although she had ceased to exist as an empire, she continued to exert an all-powerful influence throughout
the Oriental world, and she exerts that influence to
this day. From the farthest limits of Greece to the
heart of Russia, all the peoples of Eastern Europe,
Turks, and Greeks, Serbs and Bulgarians, Roumanians and Russians, have preserved the living memory
and the traditions of vanished Byzantium.

And so, this old story, only partially understood,
and in a measure forgotten, is not, as is too readily

thought, dead history. It has left, even to our own day, deep traces in the progress of ideas and in political ambitions; it still contains promises and pledges for the future for all the nations that have inherited its possessions. It is for this reason that Byzantine civilization doubly merits attention, no less for what it was in itself, than for what remains of it in the history of our own time.

THE END

APPENDIX I

Dynasty of Constantine

Constantine I, the Great, 306–337; sole emperor, 323–337.
Constantius II, 337–361; sole emperor, 353–361.
Julian, 361–363.
Jovianus, 363–364.
Valens, 364–378.

Dynasty of Theodosius

Theodosius I, the Great, 379–395.
Arcadius, 395–408.
Theodosius II, 408–450.
Marcianus, 450–457.
Leo I, 457–474.
Zeno, 474–491.
Anastasius I, 491–518.

Dynasty of Justinian

Justin I, 518–527.
Justinian I, 527–565.
Justin II, 565–578.
Tiberius II, 578–582.
Maurice, 582–602.
Phocas (usurper), 602–610.

Dynasty of Heraclius

Heraclius, 610–641.
Constantine III, 641–642.

APPENDIX I

Constans II, 642–668.
Constantine IV, *Pogonatus*, 668–685.
Justinian II, *Rhinotmetus*, 685–695.
Leontius (usurper), 695–698.
Tiberius III (usurper), 698–705.
Justinian II (for the second time), 705–711.
Philippicus, 711–713.
Anastasius II, 713–716.
Theodosius III, 716–717.

Isaurian Dynasty

Leo III, 716–741.
Constantine V, *Copronymus*, 741–775.
Leo IV, 775–780.
Constantine VI, 780–797.
Irene, 797–802.
Nicephorus I, (usurper), 802–811.
Stauracius, 811.
Michael I, *Rhangabe*, 811–813.
Leo V, the Armenian, 813–820.
Michael II, *Balbus*, 820–829.
Theophilus, 829–842.
Michael III, the Drunkard, 842–867.

Macedonian Dynasty

Basil I, 867–886.
Leo VI, the Sage, 886–912.
Alexander, 912–913.
Constantine VII, *Porphyrogenitus*, 912–959, associated with
    Romanus I, *Lecapenus* (usurper), 919–944.
Romanus II, 959–963.
Nicephorus II Phocas, 963–969.
John I Tzimisces, 969–976.
Basil II, *Bulgaroctonos*, 976–1025.
Constantine VIII, 1025–1028.

APPENDIX I

Zoe, 1028–1050; associated with her successive husbands:
Romanus III, *Argyrus*, 1028–1034;
Michael IV, the Paphlagonian, 1034–1041;
Michael V, *Calaphates* (adopted by Zoe), 1041–1042.
Constantine IX, *Monomachus*, 1042–1054; and with
Theodora, 1054–1056.
Michael VI, *Stratioticus*, 1056, 1057.

Dynasty of the Ducases and the Comneni

Isaac I Comnenus, 1057–1059.
Constantine X Ducas, 1059–1067.
Romanus IV, *Diogenes*, 1067–1071.
Michael VII Ducas, 1071–1078.
Nicephorus III, *Botaniates* (usurper), 1078–1081.
Alexius I Comnenus, 1081–1118.
John II Comnenus, 1118–1143.
Manuel I Comnenus, 1143–1180.
Alexius II Comnenus, 1180–1183.
Andronicus I Comnenus, 1183–1185.

Dynasty of the Angeli

Isaac II, 1185–1195.
Alexius III, 1195–1203.
Isaac II (the second time) associated with his son Alexius IV,
1203–1204.
Alexius V, *Murtzuphlos* (usurper), 1204.

Latin Emperors of Constantinople

Baldwin of Flanders, 1204–1205.
Henry of Flanders, 1206–1216.
Peter of Courtenay, 1217.
Yolande, 1217–1219.
Robert II of Courtenay, 1221–1228.
Baldwin II, 1228–1261, assisted by John of Brienne as regent,
1229–1237; sole emperor, 1240–1261.

APPENDIX I

Greek Emperors of Nicæa

Theodore I Lascaris, 1204–1222.
John III Vatatzes, 1222–1254.
Theodore II Lascaris, 1254–1258.
John IV Lascaris, 1258–1259.
Michael VIII Palæologus (usurper), 1259–1261.

Dynasty of the Palæologi

Michael VIII, 1261–1282.
Andronicus II, 1282–1328, associated with his son Michael IX, 1295–1320.
Andronicus III, 1328–1341.
John V, 1341–1376.
John VI Cantacuzene (usurper), 1341–1355.
Andronicus IV (son of John V), 1376–1379.
John V (for the second time), 1379–1391.
John VII (son of Andronicus IV; usurper), 1390.
Manuel II, 1391–1425.
John VIII, 1425–1448.
Constantine XIII Palæologus, 1448–1453.

Greek Despots of Mistra

Manuel Cantacuzene, 1348–1380.
Matthew Cantacuzene, 1380–1383.
Theodore I Palæologus, 1383–1407.
Theodore II, 1407–1443.
Constantine Dragases, 1428–1448.
Thomas, 1432–1460.
Demetrius, 1449–1460.

APPENDIX II

CHRONOLOGICAL TABLE OF THE MOST IMPORTANT
EVENTS IN BYZANTINE HISTORY

330 May 11. Founding of Constantinople, "New Rome," by
Constantine the Great.

343 Council of Sardica.

351 Battle of Mursa.

353 Constantius sole emperor.

359 Council of Rimini.

376 Establishment of the Visigoths in Mœsia.

378 Battle of Adrianople, and death of the Emperor Valens.

381 Œcumenical council of Constantinople.

395 Death of Theodosius. Division of the empire between his
sons Arcadius and Honorius.

396 Invasion of Greece by Alaric. The Visigoths surrounded
by Stilicho at Pholoe.

399–400 Revolt of Gainas.

404 Deposition and exile of St. John Chrysostom.

410 Capture of Rome by Alaric.

431 Œcumenical council of Ephesus.

438 Promulgation of the Theodosian Code.

439 Great Wall of Constantinople built.

441 Invasion of Pannonia by Attila.

447 New invasion by Attila.

449 Council called the "Robber Council of Ephesus."

451 Œcumenical council of Chalcedon.

476 Fall of the Roman Empire of the West.

482 Edict of Union, or "Henotikon."

487 Theodoric, King of the Ostrogoths, commissioned by
Zeno to reconquer Italy.

APPENDIX II

502 Renewal of war with the Persians.

512 Wall of Anastasius built.

514 Revolt of Vitalian.

519 Reëstablishment of union with Rome, and end of the schism of Acacius (484–519).

527 Renewal of the war against the Persians.

529 Promulgation of the Justinian Code.

529 Closing of the Schools of Athens.

532 Perpetual peace concluded with the Persians.

532 The *Nika* Revolt.

533 Publication of the *Digest* and *Institutes*.

533–534 Belisarius reconquers Africa.

535 *Novels* of Justinian, for the administrative reorganization of the Empire.

535 War against the Ostrogoths.

536 Council of Constantinople.

537 First service in Saint Sophia.

537–538 Siege of Rome; the city defended by Belisarius.

540 Capture of Ravenna by Belisarius.

540 Khusrau invades Syria.

540 Invasion of Illyricum by the Huns.

543 Edict of Justinian concerning the Three Chapters.

548 Death of Theodora.

549 Rome retaken by Totila.

552 Defeat of the Ostrogoths at Taginæ, and end of the Ostrogothic Kingdom.

553 Œcumenical council of Constantinople.

554 Conquest of southeastern Spain.

559 The Huns before Constantinople.

562 Peace with Persia.

568 Invasion of Italy by the Lombards.

572 Renewal of war with the Persians.

579 Death of Khusrau the Great.

581 Capture of Sirmium by the Avars.

Circa 582 Creation of the Exarchates of Africa and of Ravenna.

591 Peace with Persia.

APPENDIX II

601 Victories of Priscus over the Avars.

602 Revolt of Phocas.

608 The Persians conquer Syria, and advance to Chalcedon.

610 Revolt of Heraclius, and fall of Phocas.

615 Capture of Jerusalem by the Persians.

617 Conquest of Egypt by the Persians.

622 Heraclius takes the offensive against the Persians.

626 The Avars and the Persians attack Constantinople.

627 Battle of Nineveh.

629 Peace with the Persians.

Early in Seventh Century. Settlement of Croats and Serbs in Illyricum.

634 The Arabs invade Syria.

636 Battle of Cadesia.

637 Surrender of Jerusalem.

638 Heraclius publishes the *Ekthesis*, or Exposition of the Faith.

640–642 Conquest of Egypt by the Arabs.

647 The Arabs in northern Africa.

648 Constans II publishes *The Type*.

655 Defeat of the Byzantine fleet off the coast of Lycia.

Mid-Seventh Century. Organization of the Asiatic *themes*.

668 The Arabs at Chalcedon.

673–678 Great Siege of Constantinople by the Arabs.

679 Settlements of the Bulgars south of the Danube.

680–681 Œcumenical council of Constantinople.

692 Defeat of Justinian II by the Arabs, at Sebastopolis.

697–698 Capture of Carthage by the Arabs, and loss of Africa.

708–Expedition of Justinian II against the Bulgars arrested.

710 Insurrection in Italy.

712–717 Advance of the Arabs in Asia Minor.

717–718 Siege of Constantinople by the Arabs.

726 Edict against the Images.

727 Insurrection in Greece and Italy.

739 Battle of Akroinon.

740 Publication of the *Ecloga*.

751 Capture of Ravenna by the Lombards.

APPENDIX II

752 Victory over the Arabs.

753 Iconoclastic Council of Hieria.

754 Gift of Pippin to the papacy. Loss of Byzantine Italy.

755 War with the Bulgars.

762 Defeat of the Bulgars at Anchialus.

765 Persecution of the defenders of Images.

787 Œcumenical council of Nicæa.

797 Constantine VI deposed by Irene.

800 Reconstruction of the Roman Empire of the West.

809 Invasion of Krum, the Bulgar Khan.

811 The Emperor Nicephorus killed in the war with Bulgars.

813 Krum before Constantinople.

815 Iconoclastic Synod of Constantinople.

817 Victory of the Byzantines at Mesembria.

822 Insurrection of Thomas.

826 Conquest of Crete by the Arabs.

827 The Arabs in Sicily.

832 Edict of Theophilus against the Images.

838 Capture of Amorion by the Arabs.

842 Capture of Messina by the Arabs.

843 Council of Constantinople, and restoration of the orthodox faith.

858 Deposition of Ignatius. Photius elected Patriarch.

863 Mission of Cyril and Methodius to the Moravians.

864 Conversion of Bulgaria.

867 Synod of Constantinople. Break with Rome.

869 Œcumenical Council of Constantinople.

876 Capture of Bari by the Greeks.

878 Capture of Syracuse by the Arabs.

879 Council of Constantinople.

887-893 Publication of the *Basilica*.

893 Break with Symeon, the Bulgarian Tsar.

902 Capture of Taormina by the Arabs. Loss of Sicily.

904 Thessalonica captured by the Arabs.

915 Battle of the Garigliano.

917 Victory of the Bulgars at Anchialus.

919 Usurpation of Romanus Lecapenus.

924 Symeon before Constantinople.
927 Death of the Tsar Symeon.
934 Capture of Melitene by the Byzantines.
944 Capture of Nisibis and Edessa.
944 Fall of Romanus Lecapenus.
961 Capture of Crete by Nicephorus Phocas.
963 Usurpation of Nicephorus Phocas.
965 Conquest of Cilicia.
967 Resumption of the Bulgarian war.
968 The Russians in Bulgaria.
968 Capture of Antioch.
969 Assassination of Nicephorus Phocas.
971 Insurrection of Bardas Phocas.
971 Defeat of the Russians at Silistria. Annexation of Bulgaria.
976 Campaign of Tzimisces in Syria.
976–979 Revolt of Bardas Scleros.
977–986 Advance of Samuel, the Bulgarian Tsar.
986 Defeat of the Greeks at the pass of the Trajan Gate.
987–989 Revolt of Bardas Phocas.
989 Conversion of Russia.
995 Campaign of Basil II in Syria.
996 Defeat of the Bulgars on the Sperchius.
998 Campaigns in Syria.
1000–1014 War against the Bulgars.
1010 Revolt of Southern Italy.
1014 Battle of Cimbalongu (Belasitza). Death of the Tsar Samuel.
1018 Submission of Bulgaria.
1018 Victory of Cannes.
1021–1022 Annexation of Armenia.
1032 Capture of Edessa by the Greeks.
1038 Success of George Maniakes in Sicily.
1040 Insurrection of Bulgaria.
1042 Revolution in Constantinople. Fall of Michael V.
1043 Revolt of George Maniakes.
1054 The Patriarch Cerularius breaks with Rome.

APPENDIX II

1057 Revolt of Isaac Comnenus.
1064 Capture of Ani by the Seljuk Turks.
1071 Capture of Bari by the Normans, and loss of Italy.
1071 Battle of Manzikert.
1078 Revolt of Bryennius and Botoniates.
1078 The Turks at Nicæa.
1081–1084 Invasion of Epirus by Robert Guiscard.
1082 Treaty with Venice.
1091 Defeat of the Petchenegs on the Leburnium.
1096 The Crusaders at Constantinople.
1097 Capture of Nicæa by the Crusaders.
1107–1108 War with Bohemond.
1116 Battle of Philomelium.
1122 Defeat of the Petchenegs.
1122–1126 War with Venice.
1124–1126 Intervention in Hungary.
1137–1138 Campaign of John Comnenus in Cilicia and Syria.
1147 The Second Crusade.
1147–1149 War with Roger II, King of Sicily.
1151 The Byzantines at Ancona.
1152–1154 War with Hungary.
1158 Campaign of Manuel Comnenus in Syria.
1168 Annexation of Dalmatia.
1171 Break with Venice.
1176 Battle of Myriokephalon.
1182 Revolt of Andronicus Comnenus.
1185 Capture of Thessalonica by the Normans.
1185 Foundation of the Wallachian-Bulgarian Empire.
1189 Frederic Barbarossa in the Orient.
1190 Isaac Angelus defeated by the Bulgars.
1197–1207 Johannitsa, the Bulgarian Tsar.
1204 Capture of Constantinople by the Latins. Foundation of
　　　 the Latin Empire of Constantinople.
1205 Defeat of the Latins at Adrianople.
1206 Theodore Lascaris crowned Emperor at Nicæa.
1210 Parliament of Ravennika.
1222 Recapture of Thessalonica by the Greeks of Epirus.

APPENDIX II

1230   Destruction of the Greek Empire of Thessalonica by the Bulgars.

1236   Constantinople attacked by the Greeks and Bulgars.

1244   The Despotat of Thessalonica becomes a vassal of Nicæa.

1254   Submission of Michael, the Despot of Epirus.

1259   Battle of Pelagonia.

1261   Treaty of Nymphæum.

1261   Recapture of Constantinople by the Greeks.

1262   The Byzantines regain a foothold in Morea.

1267–1272   Advance of Charles of Anjou in Epirus.

1274   Council of Lyons.

1281   Victory of Berat over the Angevin troops.

1302–1311   The Catalan Grand Company in the Orient.

1311   Battle of Lake Copais.

1326   Capture of Brusa by the Turks.

1325–1328   War of the two Andronici.

1330   The Bulgars beaten by the Serbs at Velbujd.

1340   Advance of the Serbs in Epirus, and of the Turks in Asia.

1341   Revolt of John Cantacuzene.

1342–1349   Revolution of the Zelots at Thessalonica.

1341–1351   Quarrel of the Hesychasts.

1345   Stephen Dushan conquers Macedonia.

1346   Coronation of Stephen Dushan as Emperor, at Uskub.

1347   Cantacuzene captures Constantinople.

1348   Foundation of the Despotat of Mistra.

1354   The Turks at Gallipoli.

1355   Death of Stephen Dushan.

1365   The Turks establish their capital at Adrianople.

1371   Battle of the Maritza.

1373   John V Palæologus vassal of the Sultan.

1376   Revolt of Andronicus IV.

1389   Battle of Kossovo.

1390   Revolt of John VII.

1391   Capture of Philadelphia by the Turks.

1396   Crusade of Nicopolis.

1397   Bajazet attacks Constantinople.

APPENDIX II

1402   Battle of Angora.
1422   Siege of Constantinople by the Turks.
1423   Thessalonica sold to Venice.
1423   Expedition of the Turks in Morea.
1430   Capture of Thessalonica by the Turks.
1439   Council of Florence.
1444   Battle of Varna.
1446   Turkish invasion in Morea.
1451   Accession of Mohammed II.
1453, May 29 Capture of Constantinople by the Turks.

APPENDIX III

CONDENSED BIBLIOGRAPHY OF THE PRINCIPAL WORKS
FOR READING OR REFERENCE

General History of the Byzantine Empire

AT present, there is no general history,—except, perhaps, in Russia,—both detailed and complete, of the Byzantine Empire, which can be said to have kept abreast of the latest scientific studies. Gibbon's work, *The History of the Decline and Fall of the Roman Empire*, is extraordinarily partial and out of date; the new edition of Bury (London, 1896, in 7 volumes) is especially valuable for the excellent notes supplied by the editor. Finlay's book, *History of Greece from its Conquest by the Romans to the Present Time* (new edition by Tozer, in 7 volumes, Oxford, 1877), as well as the more condensed work of Hertzberg: *Geschichte der Byzantiner und des osmanischen Reiches bis gegen Ende des XVI Jahrhunderts* (Berlin, 1883), was written before the great scientific researches of recent years; and if Charles Hopf's work, published in Ersch and Gruber's *Encyclopædia* (vols. 85 and 86), under the title: *Geschichte Griechenlands vom Beginn des Mittelalters bis auf unsere Zeit* (1867), deserves always to be consulted, it is chiefly valuable for the period following the fourth Crusade, and for the history of the Latin states founded in Greece after 1204. Muralt's *Chronographie Byzantine* (St. Petersburg, 1855–1873, 2 vols.) despite many errors, is always a useful chronological repertory.

In recent years, several Russian scholars have begun to publish general histories of Byzantium. That of Koulakovski (Kiev, 1910–1915) comprises three volumes, which recount the events from 395 to 717. The work of Ouspenski (Petrograd, 1913) is in a single volume, and also stops at 717. That of Vassilief (Petro grad, 1917), covers in its first volume the period from the fourth century to 1081. Finally, one must cite the Ἱστορία τῆς Ἑλλάδος of Lambros, of which volumes III to VI (Athens, 1892–1908) tell the story of the Empire from Constantine to 1453.

In default of a general history of Byzantium, there are some short manuals of which the best are: Gelzer, *Abriss der byzantinischen Kaisergeschichte* (Munich, 1897, at the end of the *Geschichte der byzantinische Litteratur*, by Krumbacher); Jorga, *The Byzantine Empire* (London, 1907); and Foord, *The Byzantine Empire* (London, 1911).

Monographs on Byzantine History

ON the other hand, we have many works covering more or less extensive periods of the history of Byzantium. The most important are:—

For the period from the end of the fourth century to the end of the ninth: Bury, *A History of the Later Roman Empire, from Arcadius to Irene* (London, 1889, 2 vols.); Diehl, *Justinien et la civilisation byzantine au VIe siècle* (Paris, 1901); Pernice, *L'imperatore Eraclio* (Florence, 1905); Schwarzlose, *Der Bilderstreit* (Gotha, 1890); Bréhier, *La querelle des images* (Paris, 1904); Lombard, *Constantin V, empereur des Romains* (Paris, 1902); Bury, *History of the Eastern Roman Empire*, 800–867, (London, 1912).

For the period from the end of the ninth century to the beginning of the thirteenth: Vogt, *Basile I* (Paris, 1908); Rambaud, *L'Empire grec au Xe siècle* (Paris, 1870); Schlumberger, *Nicéphore Phocas* (Paris, 1890); *L'épopée byzantine à la fin du Xe siècle*, 969–1057 (Paris, 1896–1905, 3 vols.); Bréhier, *Le schisme oriental du XIe siècle* (Paris, 1899); Neumann, *Die Weltstellung des byzantinischen Reiches vor den Kreuzzügen* (Leipzig, 1894; French translation, Paris, 1905); Chalandon, *Essai sur le règne d'Alexis Comnène* (Paris, 1900); *Jean II Comnène et Manuel Comnène* (Paris, 1912); Cognasso, *Partiti politici e lotte dinastiche in Bisanzio* (Turin, 1912); Isaac Ange *Bessarione*, 1915; Luchaire, *Innocent III: la question d'Orient* (Paris, 1907); Norden, *Der vierte Kreuzzug* (Berlin, 1898).

APPENDIX III

For the period from 1204 to 1453: Gerland, *Geschichte des lateinischen Kaiserreiches* (Hamburg, 1905); Miliarakis, Ἱστορία τοῦ Βασιλείου τῆς Νικαίας (Athens, 1898); Gardner, *The Lascarids of Nicæa* (London, 1913); Buchon, *Recherches sur la principauté franque de Morée* (Paris, 1841–1846, 5 vols.); Rennell Rodd, *The Princes of Achaia* (London, 1907, 2 vols.); Miller, *The Latins in the Levant* (London, 1908); Schlumberger, *Expédition des Almugavares* (Paris, 1902); Berger de Xivrey, *Manuel II Paléologue* (Paris, 1853); Schlumberger, *La prise de Constantinople* (Paris, 1914); Fallmerayer, *Geschichte des Kaisertums Trapezunt* (Munich, 1827).

We must not omit to mention, in addition, several monographs relative to the history of certain provinces or cities: Diehl, *L'Afrique byzantine* (Paris, 1896); *Études sur l'administration byzantine dans l'exarchat de Ravenne* (Paris, 1888); Gay, *L'Italie méridionale et l'empire byzantin*, 867–1071 (Paris, 1904); Gregorovius, *Geschichte der Stadt Athen in Mittelalter* (Stuttgart, 1889, 2 vols.); Tafrali, *Thessalonique au XIVe siècle* (Paris, 1912); Diehl, *Venise, une république patricienne* (Paris, 1915).

Among the monographs devoted to certain notable persons should be named: Hergenrother, *Photius* (Regensburg, 1867–1869, 3 vols.); Diehl, *Théodora* (Paris, 1904), and *Figures byzantines* (Paris, 1906 and 1908, 2 vols.); Rambaud, *Psellos* (in *Études sur l'histoire byzantine* Paris, 1912); Vast, *Le cardinal Bessarion* (Paris, 1897).

For the history of the people associated with the Greek Empire: Jirecek, *Geschichte der Bulgaren* (Prague, 1876); *Geschichte der Serben*, vol. 1 (Gotha, 1911); Jorga, *Geschichte des osmanischen Reichs*, vols. 1 and 11 (Gotha, 1908–1909).

Finally, for the general history of Byzantium, we will cite the most recent work: Diehl, *Byzance, grandeur et décadence* (Paris, 1919).

Religious History

Gasquet, *De l'autorité impériale en matière de religion* (Paris, 1879); Pargoire, *L'Église byzantine de 527 à 847* (Paris, 1905); Norden, *Das Papsttum und Byzanz* (Berlin, 1903).

APPENDIX III

Administrative History of the Empire

Diehl, *Études byzantines* (Paris, 1905); Gelzer, *Die Genesis der byzantinische Themenverfassung* (Leipzig, 1899); Bury, *The Imperial Administrative System in the Ninth Century* (London, 1910); Schlumberger, *Sigillographie byzantine* (Paris, 1884).

History of Byzantine Civilization

Paparrigopoulo, *Histoire de la civilisation hellénique* (Paris, 1878); Hesseling, *Essai sur la civilisation byzantine* (Paris, 1907); Turchi, *La civiltà bisantina* (Florence, 1910).—For the history of law: Zachariae de Lingenthal, *Geschichte des griechisch-römischen Rechts* (3d edition, Berlin, 1892).—For the history of commerce: Heyd, *Histoire du commerce du Levant au moyen-âge* (Leipzig, 1885, 2 vols.).—For the history of literature: Krumbacher, *Geschichte der byzantinische Litteratur* (2d edition, Munich, 1897).—For the topography of Constantinople: Ducange, *Constantinopolis christiana* (Paris, 1680); Mordmann, *Esquisse topographique de Constantinople* (Lille, 1892); Ebersolt, *Le grand palais de Constantinople* (Paris, 1910).—For the history of art: Bayet, *L'art byzantin*, (2d edition, Paris, 1904); Millet, *L'art byzantin* (Paris, in A. Michel, *Histoire de l'art*, vols. I, 1905, and III, 1908); Diehl, *Manuel d'art byzantin* (Paris, 1910); Dalton, *Byzantine Art and Archæology* (Oxford, 1911).

INDEX

Names of the Eastern Emperors, from Arcadius down, are set in capitals and small capitals.

Achaia, Principality of, 138,139,149, 150,153,154.
Africa, 23,24,26,51
Africa, Exarchate of, 37,45,47,48.
Agathias, 34.
Akindynos, 158.
Alaric, King of the Visigoths, 7.
Alexander III, Pope, 127.
Alexandria, 14.
ALEXIUS (I) Comnenus, 110,112, 114,115,116,117,120,121,122,123, 124,128,129.
ALEXIUS (II) Comnenus, 132.
ALEXIUS (III) Angelus, 132,133,134, 135,138.
ALEXIUS IV, 135,136.
ALEXIUS V, 136.
Alexius I of Trebizond, 139,143,173.
Alexius II of Trebizond, 173.
Alexius III of Trebizond, 173,174.
Alp Arslan, 106.
Amalasuntha, 24.
Amru, 43.
ANASTASIUS, 12,14,17,33.
Anatolia, 14,15.
ANDRONICUS (I) Comnenus, 113,132, 134.
ANDRONICUS (II) Palæologus, 155, 156,158,160,161,163,171.
ANDRONICUS (III) Palæologus, 155, 156,165.
ANDRONICUS (IV) Palæologus, 157.
Anna Comnena, 130.
Anne of Savoy, 156,159,161.
Anthemius of Tralles, 35.
Antioch, 14,41,79,117,123,124,125.

Arabs, 29,43,44,51,54,55,62,63,67,68, 70,77,85,86.
ARCADIUS, 6,7.
Architecture, 35,36.
Argyropulus, 169.
Arian controversy, the, 9.
Arius, 9.
Armenia, 37,79.
Art, 14,15,35,36,97,98,99,130,131, 170,171.
Artavasdus, 59.
Asen, John, Tsar of Bulgaria, 133, 144,145,146,160.
Asen, Peter, 133.
Athens, Duchy of, 149,151,165.
Athens, University of, closed by Justinian, 33.
Atteleiates, Michael, 97.
Attila, 7,8.
Avars, 27,41.

Bacon, Roger, 170.
Bajazet, 163,164.
Baldwin, Count of Flanders. *See* Baldwin I.
BALDWIN I, Latin Emperor at Constantinople, 136,138,140,142.
BALDWIN II, Latin Emperor, 144, 146,148.
Balkan Peninsula, 38,46,47,80,88, 163.
Bardas, 66,70,71.
Bardas, Cæsar, 69.
Bardas Phocas, 78,101,102.
Bardas Sclerus, 101,102.
Barlaam, 158.

INDEX

Basil, Saint, 72.
BASIL I, the Macedonian, 71 and *n*.,
72,73,78,88,93,97,100,103,104.
BASIL II, 72,75,79,80,83,84,85,86,87,
88,89,95,101,104,106,134.
Basil, Grand Chamberlain, 73,76.
Basilakes, 110.
Basileus, 90,91.
Beccus, John, Patriarch of Constan-
tinople, 154.
Bela III, of Hungary, 115,116.
Belisarius, 20,23,24,26,27.
Benjamin of Tudela, 131.
Berbers, 29,48.
Bessarion, 169,172.
Bodonitza, 138.
Bogomiles, heresy of, 82,114.
Bohemond, 106,120,123,124.
Boniface of Montferrat, King of
Thessalonica, 136,138,141.
Boris, Tsar of Bulgaria, 70.
Boucicault, Marshal, 166.
Bucelin, 25.
Bulgaria, 70,71,79–84,141,142,144,
145,152,163.
Bulgarians, 15,47,51,55,63,68,80–84,
160,161.
Bulgaroctonos (Basil II), 83.

Cabasilas, 169.
Cæsaropapism, 5.
Cantacuzene. *See* JOHN VI.
Carthage, Exarchate of. *See* Africa,
Exarchate of.
Catalan Grand Company, 160.
Cerigo, 139.
Chalcedon, Council of (451), 11,34
and *n*.
Chalcondylas, 169,172.
Charlemagne, 61,63,67.
Charles of Anjou, 153,154.
Charles Martel, 54.
Chosroes. *See* Khusrau.
Christianity, spread of, 69,70,88,89.
Christodulus, St., 129.
Chronicle of Morea, The, 149.
Chrysoloras, 169.
Chrysostom, St. John, 12.
Church, Eastern. *See* Greek Church.

Cilicia, 125.
Circus factions ("Greens and Blues"),
15,22,37,38.
Clement VI, Pope, 162.
Colchis, 27.
Conrad III of Germany, 124.
CONSTANS II, 43,44,45.
CONSTANTINE I, Roman Emperor,
and the founding of Constanti-
nople, 3–5.
CONSTANTINE IV, 44,45.
CONSTANTINE V, 53–55,59,60,61.
CONSTANTINE VI, 62,63,67.
CONSTANTINE VII, 75,76,81,96,97,
100,101,103.
CONSTANTINE VIII, 75,104.
CONSTANTINE IX, 76,94,105,107,108.
CONSTANTINE (X) Ducas, 105.
CONSTANTINE (XIII) Palæologus,
155,159,167,168.
Constantine, Patriarch of Constanti-
nople, 60.
Constantine Bodin, 115.
Constantine Phocas, 78.
Constantinople, founded, 3 *ff*.; re-
built by Justinian, 32; captured
by the Crusaders, 136, 138; re-
captured by Greeks, 148; taken
by Mohammed II, 167,168; 7,8,
14,15,29,35,44,54,68,69,70,77,94,
96,98,99,131,169–171.
Constantinople, Councils of: (381),
9; (536), 33; (556), 34; (680), 45;
(867), 71.
Constantinople, University of,69,96,
129.
CONSTANTIUS II, 9.
Consular office, suppressed by Jus-
tinian, 32.
Corpus Juris Civilis (Justinian's),
30,31,93.
Crepin, Robert, 109.
Crete, 67,77,78.
Critobulus, 169.
Croats, 42,46,47,85.
Crusades, the, and the Empire,
122 *ff*.,136,138.
Cyprus, 43,55.
Cyril, St., "Apostle of the Slavs," 69.

INDEX

Cyril, patriarch of Alexandria, 10,11.
Cyrus, patriarch of Alexandria, 42.

Damascus, 41,43.
Dandolo, Henry, Doge of Venice, 135,136,142.
David of Trebizond, 139,143,175.
Demetrius, Despot of Mistra, 175.
Demetrius Cydones, 169.
Demetrius of Montferrat, King of Thessalonica, 144,147.
Digenis Acritas, 97.
Diocletian, 3.
Dioscurus, patriarch of Alexandria, 10,11.
Dragutin (Serb), 161.
Ducas, 169.
Dushan, Stephen. *See* Stephen Dushan.

Egypt, 14,15,43,46.
Ephesus, 14.
Ephesus, Council of (431), 11; "Robber Council" of (449), 11.
Epirus, Depotat of, 139,144,146,147, 148,151,154.
Ertoghrul (Turk), 162.
Espanagoge, 93.
Eugene IV, Pope, 159.
Eustathius of Thessalonica, 130.
Eutyches, heresy of, 11.
Evagrius, 34.

Franks, 61.
Frederic I (Barbarossa), 126, 127, 134.
Frederic II, 146.

Gabalas, 139.
Gabras, 132.
Geisa II, King of Hungary, 116.
Gelimer, King of the Vandals, 23, 24.
Gemistus. *See* Plethon.
Gepidæ, 29.
Germanus, patriarch of Constantinople, 59.
Germany, invasions of barbarians from, 6–8.
Giustiniani, General, 168.

Greek, supersedes Latin as the vernacular tongue, 48,49,50.
Greek Church, becomes a State Church, 12; relations of, with the Papacy, 12,13,14,18,33,34,38,45, 51,57*ff*.,62,64*ff*.,71,107,108,127, 153,167.
Greens and Blues. *See* Circus factions.
Gregory I (the Great), Pope, 38.
Gregory II, 59.
Gregory III, 59.
Gregory X, 153.
Gregory of Nazianzus, 12.
Gregory Palamas, 158,169.
Guiscard, Robert, Duke of Apulia, 106, 120.

Harun-al-Raschid, Caliph, 63.
Hellenism, 14.
Henotikon (edict of union), effect of, 13.
HENRY of Flanders, Latin Emperor, 141,142,143.
Henry II, Holy Roman Emperor, 87.
Henry VI, 134.
HERACLIUS, founds a new dynasty, 39; 41,42,43,46,48,49.
Herulis, 29.
Hervé, 109.
Hesychasts, 158,159.
Hieria, Council of, 60.
Honorius, Western Emperor, 6.
Hungary, 114*ff*.
Huns, the, 7,8,27,38.
Hunyady, John, 164,165.

Ibas, of Edessa, 34 *n*.
Iberia, 79,80.
Iconium, Sultanate of, 117,118,119.
Iconoclastic Controversy, the, 57*ff*., 64*ff*.; consequences of, 61,67.
Images (holy), the. *See* Iconoclastic Controversy.
Innocent III, Pope, 134.
Irene, Regent, 62–64,67.
ISAAC (I) Comnenus, 105,109.
ISAAC (II) Angelus, 132*ff*., 136.
Isidore of Miletus, 35.

INDEX

Islamism, birth of, 43.
Italy, 24,25,26,61,67,85 *ff*.,105,106, 107. And *see* Venice.

Jerusalem, 41,42,43,123,126.
Jesus, controversy over nature of. *See* Eutyches, Monophysitism.
Johannitza, Tsar of Bulgaria,133,134, 141,142,144.
John I, Pope, 18.
JOHN (I) Tzimisces, 72,75,79,82,103, 104.
JOHN (II) Comnenus, 112,114,115, 117,118,121,122,124,125,128,129.
JOHN (III) Vatatzes, 143,145,146, 147.
JOHN (V) Palæologus, 155,156,157, 159,163,167.
JOHN (VI) Cantacuzene, 155,156, 157,158,159,163,169,171.
JOHN (VII) Palæologus, 157.
JOHN (VIII) Palæologus, 155,159, 167.
John (Lekanomantis), patriarch of Constantinople, 66.
John Angelus, 146.
John of Brienne, 145.
John of Cappadocia, 20.
John of Damascus, 59.
John of Ephesus, 34.
John Mauropus, 109.
JUSTIN I, 17–19,22.
JUSTIN II, 37.
JUSTINIAN I, 19–37,48,49,131.
JUSTINIAN II, 51,55.

Kairwan, 44.
Khusrau (Chosroes) I, King of Persia, 22,26,27.
Khusrau II, 39, 41.
Kiliz Arslan I, Sultan of Iconium, 117.
Kiliz Arslan II, 119.
Koloman, King of Hungary, 115.

Lazi, 29.
Legitimation, principle of, 74,75.
Lemnos, 139.
Leo I, Pope, 10,11.

Leo IX, Pope, 107.
LEO II, 8.
LEO III, 52–56; starts Iconoclastic Controversy, 57 *ff*., 61.
LEO IV, 55,62.
LEO V, 65,67.
LEO VI, 74,81,85,93,94,103.
Leo, Prince of Armenia, 125.
Leo the Deacon, 97.
Leo Phocas, 78.
Leo Sguros, 139.
Leo of Thessalonica, 69.
Leo Tornikius, 108.
Leo of Tripoli, 78.
Leontius of Byzantium, 34.
Leutharis, 25.
Literature, 96,97,130,169,170.
Lombards, 29,37,41,45,48,59,61,63.
Louis VII of France, 124.
Louis IX (Saint), 146.
Lyons, Council of, 153.

Malek Shah, 106,117.
Mancaphas, 139.
Manfred, King of Sicily, 147.
Maniakes, George, 106, 108.
MANUEL (I) Comnenus, 112,113,115, 116,118,119,121,122,124,125,126, 127,128,131,132.
MANUEL (II) Palæologus, 155,159, 167,169,172.
Manuel, Despot of Mistra, 171.
Manuel Ducas Angelus, 145.
Manuel Panselinos, 170.
MARCIANUS, 7,8.
Marcus Eugenicus, 169.
Martin I, Pope, 45.
Mary of Antioch, 126,132.
MAURICE, 37,38,47.
Melissenus, 110.
Mesopotamia, 27,43.
Methodius, "Apostle of the Slavs," 69.
MICHAEL II, 65,67.
MICHAEL III, 70,71.
MICHAEL IV, 105.
MICHAEL V, 76.
MICHAEL (VII) Ducas, 105,109,110.

INDEX

MICHAEL (VIII) Palæologus, 147, 148,150,152-155,158,160,165.
Michael, Tsar of Bulgaria, 160.
Michael II, of Epirus, 147, 148.
Michael Ceroularius, patriarch of Constantinople, 104,107,108,109.
Michaelangelo Comnenus, 139.
Milutin (Serb), 161.
Mistra, 171-173.
Moaviyah, Caliph, 44.
Mohammed II, takes Constantinople (1453), 165,167,168;172,174, 175.
Monophysites, 11,12,13,14,18,33,34 and n.,42,45.
Monothelitism, 42,45.
Morea, Despotat of, 150,151,165, 167,171-173,174,175.
Moschopulus, 169.
Murad I, 163.
Murad II, 164.

Naples, 24.
Narses, 20,24,25.
Naxos, 139.
Negropont, 138.
Neopatras, Duchy of, 151.
Nestorius, patriarch of Constantinople, 10,11.
Nicæa, Greek Emperors at, 136 ff.
Nicæa, Councils of, 9,62.
NICEPHORUS I, 64,65,68.
NICEPHORUS (II) Phocas, 72,75,78, 79,82,86,101,102,103.
NICEPHORUS III, 105,110.
Nicephorus, patriarch of Constantinople, 65,67.
Nicephorus Bryennius, 110,130.
Nicephorus Chumnos, 169.
Nicephorus Gregoras, 169.
Nicetas Acominatus, 130.
Nicholas I, Pope, 70,71.
Nicholas, patriarch of Constantinople, 74,103.
Nika, the (popular revolt), 22,23.
Normans, 105,106.

Olga, Tsarina of Russia, 89.
Omar, Caliph, 43.

Ommiad caliphs, 44.
Orkhan (Turk), 162,163.
Osman (Turk), 162.
Osmanli Turks, 162,163.
Ostrogoths, 8,24,25.
Otto I, 86.
Otto II, 87.
Ouzoun Hassan, Prince, 175.

Papacy, temporal domain of, 61. And see Greek Church.
Patmos, monastery of, 129.
Patriarchs of Constantinople, power of, 103.
Paul the Silentiary, 34.
Paulician heresy, 69.
Pepin, King of the Franks, 61.
Persians, 15,22,26,27,37,38,39,41.
Petchenegs, 105,114,115.
Peter, Tsar of Bulgaria, 82.
Peter Delcanus, 105.
PHOCAS (usurper), 38,39.
Photius, patriarch of Constantinople, 70,71,97,104.
Phrantzes, 169.
Planudes, 169.
Plethon Gemistus, 169,172.
Polyeuctes, patriarch of Constantinople, 103.
Prefectures of the prætorium, 13.
Prochiros Nomos, 93.
Procopius, 21,29,34.
Psellus, 97,109.
Pulcheria, 10.

Rascia (Serbia), 115.
Ravenna, Exarchate of, 37,45,48,61.
Raymond, Prince of Antioch, 125.
Religious controversies, 9 ff., 33,34, 38,42,45,57 ff.,62,64 ff.,102-104, 154,158,159.
Renard, Prince of Antioch, 125.
Rhodes, 44,145.
Rimini, Council of, 9.
Robert, Latin Emperor at Constantinople, 144.
Roger II, King of the Two Sicilies, 120,121.

INDEX

Roman Empire, separation of into Western and Eastern Empires, 5,6.
Romanos, 35.
ROMANUS (I) Lecapenus, 72,73,75, 79,81,100.
ROMANUS II, 75,76,101.
ROMANUS III, 105.
ROMANUS IV, 105,106,109.
Rome, 24. And *see* Greek Church, Papacy.
Roussel of Bailleul, 109.
Russia, 88,89.
Russians, 70,82.

Saladin, 119.
Samuel, Tsar of Bulgaria, 83,84.
Santorin, 139.
Scanderbeg, 164.
Scholarius, George, 169.
Sciences, the, 169,170.
Sclerus. *See* Bardas Sclerus.
Scylitzes, 97.
Seljuk Turks, 106,107,116,117,143.
Serbia, 114,115,116,133,152,161,162, 163.
Serbs, 42,46,47,160.
Sergius, patriarch of Constantinople, 41,42.
Sicilian Vespers, 154.
Sicily, 24,44,67,68,85. And *see* Two Sicilies.
Simeon Magistros, 97.
Sischman, Count, 83.
Slavs, 15,27,38,47,51.
Soliman, Emir, 116,117.
Spain, 25,41.
Stephen, St., the Younger, 60.
Stephen II, Pope, 61.
Stephen III, of Hungary, 116.
Stephen Dushan, 161,162.
Stephen Nemanya, 116,133,161.
Stilicho Flavius, 7.
Sviatoslaff, Prince of Kiev, 82.
Symeon, Tsar of Bulgaria, 80,81.
Syria, 14,15,27,43.

Tancred, 124.
Tarasius, patriarch of Constantinople, 62.

Terbel, Bulgar Khan, 51.
Themes, Empire divided into, 48.
Theodahad, 24.
Theodora, Justinian's Empress, 20–22,23,33,34.
Theodora (widow of Theophilus), Regent, 66,70.
THEODORA (niece of BASIL II), Empress, 75,105.
Theodore, Abbot, 65.
Theodore Ducas Angelus, 144,145.
THEODORE LASCARIS I (at Nicæa), 139,142,143.
THEODORE LASCARIS II (at Nicæa), 147.
Theodore Metochite, 169.
Theodore of Mopsuestia, 34 *n.*
Theodore Prodromus, 130.
Theodore of Studion, 63,66.
Theodoret of Cyrrhus, 34 *n.*
Theodoric, King of the Ostrogoths, 8,24.
Theodosian Code, 10.
Theodosius I (the Great), Roman Emperor, 6,7,9.
THEODOSIUS II, 10.
Theophano, 87.
Theophanus, 44.
THEOPHILUS, 65,66,68.
Thessalonica, 134,136,138,141,145, 147,157,158,162,163,164.
Thomas, 67.
Thomas, Despot of the Morea, 174.
"Three Chapters, The," 34 and *n.*
TIBERIUS, 37.
Timur, 164.
Toghrul Beg, 106.
Totila (Ostrogoth), 24.
Trebizond, Empire of, 139,151,173, 174,175.
Tribonian, 20,30.
Triklinius, 169.
Turks. *See* Osmanli Turks, Seljuk Turks.
Two Sicilies, Kingdom of, 120,121, 122.
Tzachas, Emir, 117.
Tzani, 29.

INDEX

Urosh I, of Serbia, 161.

Valens, Roman Emperor, 7.
Vandal kingdom in Africa, 23,24.
Varna, battle of, 164,166.
Venice, 61,67,88,106,120,121,122, 134,135,136,139,141,142,148,149, 153,165,166.
Vigilius, Pope, 34.
Villehardouin, Geoffrey I of, 131,138, 139,141,149.
Villehardouin, Geoffrey II of, 149.
Villehardouin, William of, Prince of Achaia, 146,147,149,150,154,171.
Visigoths, 6,7.
Vitalianus, 16,18.

Vitiges, King of the Ostrogoths, 24.
Vladimir, Prince of Kiev, 89.

Wallachia, Greater. *See* Neopatras.
Wallachian-Bulgarian Empire, 133, 134,160.
William I, of the Two Sicilies, 121, 122.
William of Champlitte, 138,139.

Xiphilin, 109.

Yaroslaff, Prince of Kiev, 89.

ZENO, 8,12,13,33.
Zoë, Empress, 75,76,104.